Prophets of Tomorrow

Prophets of Tomorrow

Spiritual Leaders for the Digital Age

Liora Ben-Sorrel

Mindful Pages

Published in 2026

ISBN: 9789374597125 (PB)
ISBN: 9789374595558 (eBook)

Published by

Mindful Pages
Imprint of Alpha Editions LLC
312 W. 2nd St #1834
Casper, WY 82601, USA

This book was developed using advanced writing tools to support the drafting and ideation process. All content has been thoughtfully curated, refined, and reviewed to ensure quality and relevance.

Content

Introduction

A teenager sits cross-legged on a bedroom floor, the dim blue light of a cheap ring lamp softening the edges of posters and half-folded laundry. With a single swipe, they open a camera, speak a few earnest sentences into the lens, and within hours their words stream across continents. Thousands listen. Hundreds respond. By the end of the night, more people have heard that brief reflection than once gathered in a village square to hear the oldest and wisest elder speak across an entire season. The miracle is palpable: a voice that might once have remained private now travels with the speed of lightning and the intimacy of a whisper. Yet there is a tremor beneath the marvel, a question we rarely pause to interrogate. What happens when reach outpaces depth, and influence expands faster than the character of the one who wields it?

The paradox is so familiar that we forget to see it. We celebrate the accessibility of voice while quietly fearing its volatility. The ancient work of guiding souls, shaping ethical imaginations, and caring for communities now takes place on platforms designed not for contemplation but for velocity. A message once sharpened through slow apprenticeship must now compete with an algorithm's appetite for novelty. The result is a new spiritual landscape, one where profound yearning meets unforgiving pace. The teenager with the camera may speak hope, truth, or wisdom—but they must do so in a space constructed to flatten nuance and reward the provocative over the measured. What was once a pulpit, raised and crafted with communal deliberation, has been replaced by a feed in which every post is both sermon and spectacle.

This book begins in that tension. It asks how we might learn to lead with substance in spaces that often feel weightless, how we might cultivate communities that nurture character rather than churn metrics, and how we might reimagine digital influence not as a cheapened imitation of spiritual authority but as a historically unprecedented form of it. For influence, in the deepest sense, was never merely about who listens. It was about who is changed.

Across cultures and millennia, spiritual leadership has always emerged in response to the needs of a people. In marketplaces and monasteries, on mountainsides and in underground gatherings, voices rose to interpret the world, challenge its injustices, and bind communities together through shared meaning. Such leadership required resilience, humility, and a profound attentiveness to human frailty. It demanded time. It demanded apprenticeship. Above all, it demanded an understanding that a leader's first task was not to gather followers but to craft the conditions in which individuals could grow into their own integrity. This ethic has not vanished. But it now competes with a technological environment that treats attention as currency, identity as brand, and influence as a perpetual performance.

To lead well in this environment requires more than strategic advice; it requires a reframing of what leadership itself means. The digital age has quietly democratised the pulpit. Everyone with a device carries a potential platform. Everyone with a story can gather a crowd. The resulting landscape is not merely noisy; it is structurally different from any communication ecosystem humanity has known. Where once ideas travelled by intentional transmission, they now travel by algorithmic propulsion. What spreads is not necessarily what is needed, but what is rewarded. And what is rewarded is what keeps people watching.

This is not a lament for a lost world, nor a nostalgic defence of institutions that often failed to live up to their responsibilities. Rather, it is a call to recognise the moment we inhabit with clarity and courage. The challenge of our time is to match the unprecedented scale of digital reach with an equally unprecedented depth of moral imagination. We cannot afford to be naïve about the forces that shape our interactions. Platforms are not neutral stages; they are engineered environments that influence not only what we see but how we think, how we relate, and how we understand ourselves. The teenager with the camera does not simply speak into a void. They speak into a system of incentives, pressures, and unspoken expectations that coax certain behaviours and constrain others. Without awareness, even the most earnest leader can drift into patterns that hollow their message and exhaust their spirit.

Throughout this book, a single motif recurs: the feed as a liturgical space. This may seem an unlikely comparison, but it is instructive. Liturgies, in their broadest sense, are repeated practices that form us, often without our conscious recognition. They nudge our desires, shape our priorities, and cultivate our attention. The scroll through a digital feed functions similarly. It trains us in habits of reaction rather than reflection, immediacy rather than discernment. To lead on these platforms is therefore to act liturgically, whether one intends to or not. The question is whether the liturgies we participate in—and create—are shaping communities for the good or merely reinforcing the restless churn of the digital economy.

The rise of digital spiritual leadership is not simply a cultural trend; it is an anthropological shift. People are no longer seeking meaning exclusively in traditional institutions. They are seeking it in livestreams, comment threads, group chats, podcasts, and short-form videos. They are gathering in dispersed yet intimate communities bonded not by geography but by shared resonance. They are asking ancient questions—about purpose, justice, suffering, belonging—but they are asking them in public, in real time, and often in front of an unseen audience. The leaders who speak into these spaces carry enormous influence, often without formal training or established accountability. This is both a gift and a peril. A gift, because new voices have the chance to speak life into places where old systems once closed doors. A peril, because the emotional, ethical, and spiritual weight of such leadership is often underestimated.

A central concern of this book is how to steward that influence responsibly. Influence is not inherently virtuous. It requires cultivation. It requires grounding. The ease of speaking to thousands does not grant the wisdom to guide them. Yet neither does a traditional title or credential guarantee depth. Authority in the digital age emerges from consistency, integrity, transparency, and an alignment between message and manner of life. It is relational authority, constantly re-affirmed through the ways leaders show up in public and private, in moments of clarity and moments of uncertainty.

The digital world magnifies this dynamic. A single misjudged phrase can unravel trust. A performative display of vulnerability can cheapen genuine connection. A relentless pursuit of engagement can distort a leader's sense of calling. Platforms reward constant visibility, yet leadership requires intervals of invisibility—moments of study, silence, and inner reckoning. The tension between presence and withdrawal lies at the heart of sustainable digital leadership. A platform may demand constant output, but a leader must resist such demands if they hope to offer wisdom rather than noise.

One of the questions this book returns to repeatedly is how leaders can create environments that form character rather than merely stimulate emotion. Emotional resonance is powerful, but it is transient. Character formation is slow, but it endures. The challenge is to use platforms designed for immediacy to nurture processes that require patience. This requires deliberate choices: designing content that encourages reflection rather than reaction; establishing rhythms that honour rest as much as productivity; cultivating spaces where disagreement can occur without humiliation; and building communities whose identity is defined not by the charisma of the leader but by shared practices of care, accountability, and discernment.

At the heart of this approach lies an insistence that digital leadership is not fundamentally about personal expression. It is about communal responsibility. The measure of a leader is not their popularity but the quality of the communities they help to sustain. A large following can be a fragile thing—volatile, fickle, and easily manipulated. A healthy community, by contrast, is a living ecosystem: shaped by rituals, fortified by trust, and animated by a shared commitment to growth. This book explores how such communities can be cultivated in digital spaces without surrendering to the performative pressures that often distort them.

As the chapters unfold, we will examine how platforms shape our attention, how algorithms influence what becomes doctrine, how performance can masquerade as authenticity, how conflicts erupt and heal online, and how power can be wielded with integrity rather than exploitation. We will look honestly at the pitfalls and seductions of digital influence—its potential to inflate ego, erode boundaries, and obscure the difference between service and self-promotion. Yet we will also recognise the profound possibilities at hand: the ability to cross borders, to amplify marginalised voices, to teach with creativity, and to build communities that would have been impossible a generation ago.

We stand, in many ways, at the threshold of a new era of spiritual communication. The tools we use will shape the teachings we share, and the teachings we share will shape the societies we inhabit. The stakes are high because the possibilities are vast. A single voice, grounded and wise, can ripple outward to thousands who long for guidance in a fractured world. A thoughtfully cultivated community can challenge the cynicism and loneliness that permeate so much digital interaction. A leader who resists the pressure to perform can model a way of being that reminds followers of their inherent dignity.

This book, then, is both map and companion. It offers frameworks for understanding digital platforms as moral and spiritual environments, but it also speaks to the inner life of the leader navigating them. It confronts uncomfortable truths, invites necessary self-examination, and proposes practices that can sustain leaders for the long work ahead. It recognises the fragility of influence and the need for structures that protect both leaders and communities from harm. It affirms that spiritual leadership is not diminished by the digital world; it is transformed by it, and in that transformation lies the possibility of renewal.

As you turn to the chapters that follow, you may find yourself reflecting on questions that press beyond the boundaries of technology. What does it mean to be a trustworthy voice when the world is inundated with noise? How does one maintain integrity when visibility becomes a form of currency? Can digital spaces become sites of genuine formation rather than mere consumption? And perhaps most crucially: what kind of communities do we hope to build for the generations that come after us?

These questions are not academic. They shape the future of our shared life. They shape the possibilities available to the teenager with the camera, to the elder whose wisdom now travels differently, and to every leader who seeks to speak into the swirling currents of the digital age with conviction, humility, and hope.

The pages ahead do not promise ease. They promise honesty, clarity, and a vision of leadership that grows deeper as the world grows faster. The platforms may be new, but the calling is ancient: to guide, to nourish, to protect, and to help communities become more humane rather than more efficient. The digital age offers tools our ancestors could scarcely imagine. What we make of them remains our task.

Chapter 1
Everyone Has a Pulpit

A woman stands at her kitchen counter at two in the morning, the house finally quiet, her hands wrapped around a mug gone lukewarm while her phone continues to vibrate on the chopping board beside her. She had gone live earlier that evening, offering a short reflection on perseverance to a few dozen regulars, most of whom she has never met. What began as a small circle of encouragement has swollen into hundreds of viewers—some asking for advice, some offering confessions, some arguing loudly with each other in the comment thread that sprawls beneath her words. She scrolls through the messages now, bewildered by the speed with which strangers have begun treating her as a guide. Her pulpit, if one can call it that, was built accidently: a front-facing camera, a cracked phone case, and the late-night courage that comes from speaking into a space that feels empty even as it is crowded with listening. She wonders whether she has become a leader or a placeholder for the needs of others. The truth, as with most things online, is both more complicated and more consequential.

This quiet scene is repeated in living rooms, bedrooms, buses, offices, and parks across the world. Not always with spiritual intent, but invariably with spiritual effect. Influence, once the preserve of those institutionally recognised or ritually prepared, now rests on devices held in nearly every hand. The shift is not merely technological; it is existential. The distance between private voice and public platform has collapsed into a few taps. A whisper can become a signal. A personal thought can become a communal anchor. A moment of vulnerability can become a viral sermon. We are living through an unprecedented flattening of access to public speech, one that has democratised influence even as it has destabilised its foundations.

The phrase "everyone has a pulpit" is not a metaphor stretched for provocation. It is a sober acknowledgement of the truth that digital platforms have rewritten the rules of public life. Spaces that were once carefully structured—town squares, classrooms, community halls, sanctuaries—have dissolved into feeds that operate as streets, stages, and sanctuaries all at once. Their fluidity is both liberating and disorienting. A livestream meant to hold a quiet prayer circle becomes, through the alchemy of algorithms, a gathering where devotion and debate coexist uncomfortably. The digital public square is a place where intimacy and spectacle collide, where personal reflections become public performances simply because enough people happen to be watching.

To lead within such an environment demands a new form of literacy: the capacity to read a room that is not a room, to discern tone and need through comment fragments and emojis, to sense the emotional temperature of a dispersed crowd whose faces you can neither see nor hear. It is leadership without the cues of breath, eye contact, or murmured agreement. The digital leader must develop an almost pastoral instinct for atmospheres that flicker and shift with each swipe. This is not a skill taught in traditional settings, yet it has become indispensable for anyone attempting to speak meaningfully into digital spaces that can turn suddenly reverent, hostile, or exhausted.

As the chapter unfolds, we must pause to recognise the historical weight of this shift. Public speech has always been contested ground. From the orators of ancient Athens to the preachers of medieval marketplaces, from the pamphleteers of the Enlightenment to the broadcasters of the twentieth century, every society has negotiated who may speak, to whom, and with what authority. The digital age has ruptured these patterns, not by expanding access alone but by stripping away the rituals that once prepared individuals for leadership. A calling that would once have been slowly discerned, nurtured, and affirmed is now thrust into the open the moment a post gains traction. The world sees the performance before it sees the preparation—if preparation occurs at all.

This is where vocation meets virality. The instincts that draw someone towards service—a desire to encourage, to teach, to uplift—are tested by the demands of platforms engineered for speed. A weekly reflection posted with care can begin, subtly and almost imperceptibly, to shape itself around what "works". What earns response. What appears, at least temporarily, to matter. The urgent displaces the important not through malice but through momentum. The creator becomes caught in the undertow of constant output, their centre gently eroded by the pressure to be present, relevant, and unmissable. It is a slow drift, and like all drifts, it tends to be noticed only after the shoreline has already vanished from view.

Yet this drift also reveals something deeper about authority in the digital world. Titles, credentials, and formal roles hold less sway online than they once did in physical communities. What travels across platforms is not institutional legitimacy but perceived authenticity. Authority is now bestowed not by vestments or official recognition but by the steady accumulation of trust: tone that feels sincere, a track record of consistency, transparency in moments of uncertainty, and the humbling willingness to be corrected. A lay organiser posting regular updates from community projects may, through steady reliability, become a citywide voice more recognisable than figures whose leadership is formally sanctioned. Authority emerges horizontally rather than vertically, shaped by relationship rather than hierarchy.

This transformation carries extraordinary potential. It also carries risks. When anyone can become a leader, anyone can harm without meaning to. Influence without grounding can inflate a sense of self or distort a sense of responsibility. At the same time, traditional institutions may be tempted to dismiss digital leaders as unserious, forgetting that communities are now forming in spaces those institutions barely understand. The challenge, therefore, is not to reclaim authority for old structures but to cultivate it wisely within new ones. Authority untethered from depth becomes performative. Authority grounded in integrity becomes transformative.

Integrity, in this new landscape, is not merely a private virtue. It must be architected into the very formats a leader uses. Platforms reward immediacy and provocation; leaders must embed countervailing practices into their digital presence. It is no longer enough to state one's values in captions or disclaimers. Integrity must express itself in design choices: setting community rules before growth, enforcing boundaries consistently, resisting the temptation to exploit outrage for engagement, and crafting digital environments where people feel safe enough to think rather than pressured to react. These are not optional tasks; they are infrastructural responsibilities. Without them, communities fracture under the weight of their own velocity.

As we move further into the chapter, we will explore how digital platforms have become the new public squares, reshaping not only communication but the very nature of communal life. We will examine how vocation is strained by the economics of attention, how authority is earned and lost in spaces that blur intimacy and spectacle, and why integrity must be engineered rather than assumed. These themes are not abstract. They surface daily in the lives of creators, mentors, activists, teachers, and ordinary people who find themselves suddenly amplified by circumstances they struggle to control.

The stakes are high because the reach is vast. To speak online is to enter a decentralised arena where ideas spread with a force once reserved for institutions. A casual reflection can challenge despair. A tired comment can wound hundreds. A simple act of consistency can build a community. The question before us is not whether everyone has a pulpit—they do. The question is what they will do with it, and whether they can cultivate the wisdom, restraint, and courage to speak with depth in spaces that reward speed.

What follows in this chapter is an invitation to recognise the profound responsibilities of digital influence and to understand the conditions that shape it. We will probe the architecture of the new public square, trace the fine line between vocation and virality, and investigate the dynamics of authority and integrity in environments that blur the sacred and the mundane. These themes are not meant to overwhelm but to orient, offering a way to inhabit the digital landscape with greater clarity and conviction.

Turn the page, then, with a sense of expectancy. The pulpit has widened beyond imagination. Its audience is vast. Its pressures are immense. Yet its possibilities—if approached with humility and depth—are greater still.

The New Public Square

On 28 March 2020, St Martin-in-the-Fields, the historic church on Trafalgar Square, streamed its first lockdown-era service on YouTube. Within minutes, the camera captured a quiet incongruity: the stillness of liturgy unfolding beneath gilded arches, and beneath it a restless column of comments flickering with prayer requests, arguments, emojis, and the occasional heckle. A congregation rooted in centuries of architectural presence now coexisted with a parallel congregation dispersed across living rooms from London to Jakarta. The feed became both pew and pavement, a place where reverence and distraction mingled without apology. A room that was not a room had opened, and those guiding it had to interpret atmospheres no building could contain.

This hybrid space—half sanctuary, half street corner—has become emblematic of the digital commons. Platforms compress multiple functions into a single stream: the intimacy of a small gathering, the unpredictability of a crowd, and the spectacle of a public stage. They are theatres without curtains, chapels without walls, and marketplaces without vendors' stalls. Leaders entering these environments must learn to "read" the collective mood through indirect cues: the speed of comments, the presence of bots, the way a single sceptical message reshapes the thread's emotional temperature. Silence can indicate absorption or abandonment. A spike in reactions may reflect encouragement or brewing conflict. This interpretive labour is subtle, continuous, and largely invisible, yet it shapes every utterance made before the lens.

The concept is not entirely novel. The Greek agora, active from at least the sixth century BCE, served as a political forum, trading hub, and religious venue simultaneously. But unlike the agora, digital platforms provide no spatial boundaries to moderate behaviour or set expectations. A livestream reflection can be a moment of collective solace and, seconds later, a stage for ideological skirmish. A prayer circle running on Instagram Live may begin with participants sharing short blessings, only for the comment stream to shift into logistical questions, private confessions, and debates about doctrine—all unfolding beneath the speaker's face. The lack of architectural cues forces leaders to construct their own sense of place through tone, ritual, and deliberate framing.

One visible behaviour illustrates this challenge. During a Ramadan livestream hosted by the Muslim Council of Britain in May 2021, the organisers paused midway through discussion to address rising tensions in the comments, where conflicting political statements had begun to dominate. They articulated community expectations succinctly, reiterated the purpose of the gathering, and introduced a brief collective reflection to recentre attention. The intervention worked; the thread stabilised and participants returned to shared focus. This episode shows how naming the space—claiming its purpose aloud—can reassemble a community momentarily frayed by the pace of digital interaction. Tone became the architecture; clarity became the boundary.

Yet not all attempts to guide the digital crowd succeed so cleanly. In July 2022, a well-known meditation teacher based in California attempted a similar recalibration during a global livestream. After a series of disruptive comments, the teacher urged viewers to hold a respectful silence. Instead, the thread fractured further, with sarcastic replies flooding in and participants debating whether the request constituted censorship. The host, trained extensively in reading physical rooms, struggled to interpret the digital atmosphere. A practice that historically relied on shared stillness collided with the platform's preference for constant motion. The teacher was not unskilled; the environment simply obeyed different rules.

Reconciling these examples points to an essential insight: the digital public square amplifies impulses that physical architecture once moderated. Behaviour spreads rapidly when the affordances of the platform—instantaneous reaction, anonymity, and minimal friction—are misaligned with the values of the gathering. Leaders must therefore treat platform design not as a neutral carrier but as a cultural force shaping collective behaviour. The digital "room" is a product of code as much as community.

This hybridity complicates authority. In traditional settings, authority rested not only on expertise but on context—the way a speaker occupied space, the collective assent implicit in showing up. Online, these cues evaporate. A comment posted halfway across the world can carry the same visual weight as a remark from someone deeply embedded in the community. The absence of agreed rituals creates a vacuum that is filled spontaneously, often by the fastest or most reactive participants rather than the most thoughtful. A leader's authority must therefore be earned continuously, not through formal recognition but through micro-behaviours visible to everyone: acknowledging difficult questions without deflection, treating disruptive voices with proportionate restraint, and showing consistency between spoken values and real-time decisions.

The public square metaphor helps, but only partially. Streets imply movement and plurality; sanctuaries imply reverence and stability. Stages imply performance and scrutiny. Digital platforms blend these metaphors so tightly that they resist disentanglement. Consider how the same livestream might host a heartfelt testimony, a heated dispute, and a casual aside about dinner within a single minute. The environment does not silo these utterances; it stacks them, revealing how different modes of expression coexist uncomfortably when context collapses. Leaders must therefore carry a dual awareness: the intention of the moment and the ambient noise of the feed.

Historical parallels offer guidance but not perfect analogies. The Reformation-era pamphlet wars of the 1520s, centred in cities like Wittenberg and Zürich, accelerated theological debate far beyond what church authorities expected. Pamphlets circulated rapidly, authorship was sometimes ambiguous, and public perception shifted faster than institutions could respond. Yet even then, influence required substantial labour: printing, distribution, and local endorsement. Today, a single video recorded in Nairobi can gather tens of thousands of views within hours. Its impact is shaped as much by platform algorithms as by the content itself. The speed compresses reflection. The scale distorts proportion.

This does not invalidate digital leadership; it redefines its demands. A conscientious leader must attend to three layers simultaneously. First, the visible content: what is said, in what tone, at what moment. Second, the visible reactions: how the audience responds, both individually and collectively. Third, the invisible architecture: how the platform's design influences what appears and how long it remains salient. Each layer influences the others. A thoughtful message may be undermined if the comment section spirals; a careful boundary-setting may falter if the platform surfaces inflammatory posts. Reading the room requires reading its code.

There is, however, a counter-example worth holding close. During the 2018 Thích Nhất Hạnh memorial vigil held online from Plum Village, France, the comment stream remained notably calm. Users repeated brief phrases of gratitude, shared memories sparingly, and responded to one another with understated kindness. No formal moderation was visible. The behaviour seemed to contradict the assumption that platforms invariably drift towards noise. The likely explanation lies in the community's longstanding shared practice: a culture of mindfulness that had been cultivated offline for decades. Participants brought that ethos with them, tempering the platform's disruptive tendencies. The environment mattered, but so did the habits participants carried into it.

This limitation refines our understanding. Platform dynamics are powerful, but not deterministic. Communities with clear identities and mature practices can bend the digital space towards their norms, at least temporarily. This does not excuse complacency; it emphasises the importance of cultivating shared language, expectations, and rituals long before crises arise. The digital public square is shaped as much by the people entering it as by the technology hosting them.

One practical measure of this shift is visible in the emergence of regular digital gatherings across faiths, activist movements, and educational initiatives. These gatherings are not mere broadcasts; they are communal experiences shaped in real time by dispersed participants. During the Black Lives Matter protests of June 2020, clergy in Minneapolis and New York used livestreamed vigils to update communities, coordinate volunteer support, and offer pastoral care. The comments mixed grief, logistics, and moral reflection. Far from diluting the message, this density revealed the multiple functions the digital public square now performs. It is a forum for information, lament, mobilisation, and debate. The leader's task is to hold these threads without losing coherence.

The quiet motif that threads through these scenes is the threshold. Platforms operate as perpetual thresholds—spaces we cross without noticing, places where identities shift, and roles blur. A viewer becomes a participant who becomes a critic within seconds. A leader speaks as a guide and is treated as a public figure whether they welcome it or not. Thresholds demand attentiveness. They reward those who recognise the transitions occurring beneath the surface.

Attending to these thresholds requires more than strategic performance. It demands a sensitivity to the emotional dynamics of digital presence: the way vulnerability circulates, the way tension escalates, the way silence can either soothe or inflame. Skilled leaders learn to detect when a community is edging towards fragmentation, when the pace of comments signals overstimulation, or when a shift in language indicates collective fatigue. These are diagnostic cues, not deterministic rules. They reflect how human behaviour adapts when stripped of the usual markers of embodiment.

Ultimately, the new public square is less a place than a practice. It is formed and reformed through millions of micro-decisions made by individuals encountering one another across distance. Its power lies in its fluidity; its danger lies in its unpredictability. For leaders, the test is not whether they can control the environment—they cannot—but whether they can interpret its patterns without surrendering their purpose to its momentum.

The unresolved tension at the centre of this subchapter is deceptively simple: when the room is not a room, how does one know when to speak, when to pause, and when to reshape the gathering altogether? The answer is neither fixed nor universal. It begins with the humility to recognise the threshold, and the courage to decide, moment by moment, how to cross it.

When Vocation Meets Virality

In January 2019, the Franciscan priest Richard Rohr sat for a podcast interview at the Centre for Action and Contemplation in Albuquerque. The conversation, recorded in a modest studio, was dense with theological reflection and careful pauses. Days later, a clipped 47-second segment—posted without his involvement—circulated widely on Instagram under a motivational caption. It gathered more than a million views within a week. Yet the fragment, stripped of the surrounding argument, conveyed a tone closer to self-help than contemplative theology. Rohr would later remark that the viral moment "was not wrong, but incomplete." His vocation had been reframed by an algorithm, the long arc of his teaching reduced to a flash. That 47-second clip shows the central tension of this subchapter: when the slow obligations of a calling collide with the furious tempo of digital attention, what remains intact and what gets quietly edited away?

The story is not unique. On 3 April 2020, the British organisation Black Cultural Archives ran a livestream discussion from its Brixton headquarters. The event intended to offer a measured historical reflection on Caribbean migration. Within hours, a ten-second excerpt featuring a passionate aside about racial solidarity was circulating independently on Twitter, gathering far more reach than the full lecture. The result was neither scandal nor success; it was distortion. A nuanced educational message became a rallying cry detached from its archival context. The comment threads, far from malicious, simply responded to the shortest, sharpest moment. Virality had identified a signal that the vocation had not meant to emphasise.

These early examples surface a motif that runs through the entire piece: the centre. A vocation seeks to hold a centre—of purpose, method, and identity. Virality pulls that centre outward, often atomising it into fragments designed for ease of consumption. The question threads beneath every paragraph: what happens when the gravitational pull of the centre weakens under the centrifugal force of content cycles?

The tension becomes visible in the behaviour of creators who begin with a weekly rhythm rooted in reflection. The pattern is familiar: a long-form piece produced every Sunday, shaped slowly, edited deliberately. Then a request for shorter material arrives—a follower asks for a clip, a colleague suggests more regular updates, or a platform rewards daily posting. The shift appears minor. But visible behaviour changes: drafts shrink, ideas are compressed, outlines turn into outlines of outlines. By the third month, the metric of success is no longer coherence but frequency. The creator's centre tilts. The urgent edges out the important.

To understand this shift with more precision, consider the case of Rabbi Danya Ruttenberg, whose 2017 thread on public accountability unexpectedly drew global attention. In interviews that followed, Ruttenberg noted that the sudden demand for daily commentary strained the deliberative pace at the heart of her rabbinic training. The visible decision to post more often produced a measurable outcome: increased reach, but decreased depth in some exchanges. The implication is clear. When vocation meets virality, the internal rhythms that give a calling its integrity can be quietly overwritten by external expectations.

A second example reinforces the pattern. In October 2021, the Singaporean interfaith educator Mohamed Imran published a series of nuanced reflections on youth radicalisation. The posts gained modest traction. But when a twenty-second clip from a public dialogue went viral, his inbox filled with requests for near-constant commentary. He complied briefly, producing daily updates. The behaviour aligned with platform incentives, yet it created a cognitive strain he later described in *The Straits Times*. The implication extended beyond personal exhaustion: the thematic centre of his work—patient education—risked diluting into reactive commentary dictated by trending topics rather than pedagogical need.

These examples might imply inevitability, but there is a counter-example worth examining. In 2020, the Quakers in Britain launched a digital series from Friends House, London. Despite moderate viral moments, they held to a strict rhythm: one reflection per week, no clips taken out of context, and no algorithm-optimised edits. The behaviour appeared counter-intuitive for growth. Yet internal audits in 2021 showed stable engagement and unusually high viewer retention. The centre held. This limitation to the virality narrative sharpens the insight rather than softens it: virality is not destiny. Structure can resist speed. The challenge is not the existence of virality but the absence of counter-rhythms to anchor vocation.

Naming the dynamic clarifies its texture. Vocation carries obligations shaped by craft, tradition, and service. These obligations require time—time to notice, to interpret, to integrate. Virality, by contrast, rewards immediacy and volume. Its metrics—views per hour, comment velocity, watch-through rates—push creators towards acceleration. When the two collide, the visible behaviours change: more posts, shorter drafts, fewer pauses, shallower revisions. The implication is not merely aesthetic but ethical. The framing of meaning shifts from fidelity to form.

The motif of the centre returns here. A centre is sustained not by sentiment but by practice: deliberate pacing, clear boundaries, and recurrent reflection. When those practices slip, even unintentionally, the centre disperses. Leaders often recognise the drift only through secondary signals: subtle anxiety before posting, reliance on engagement metrics as proxy for purpose, or an erosion in confidence about what should or should not be said. These are diagnostic cues of a vocation pulled into orbit by forces it did not choose.

Historical precedent grounds this insight. The nineteenth-century abolitionist Frederick Douglass, speaking in Ireland in 1845, wrote letters describing the difficulty of maintaining his rhetorical centre amidst rising public attention. Although far removed from digital dynamics, Douglass's reflections reveal a similar pattern: increased demand for commentary can obscure the core work of advocacy. He spoke of the risk that "the cry of the crowd may drown the needs of the cause." The behaviour he identified—pressure to respond rapidly to external demand—maps uncannily onto modern digital patterns.

Yet digital cycles add new layers. Algorithms amplify content not through discernment but through behavioural signals: retention curves, comment spikes, share rates. These metrics create subtle feedback loops. When a reflective post performs moderately but a reactive clip surges, the psychological effect is immediate. The creator feels tugged towards the trending topic, even if it sits at the periphery of their vocation. The visible decision to post about it once becomes a repeated behaviour. Over time, the centre drifts. The implication is structural: vocations require guardrails that platforms will never supply.

The tension intensifies for those whose callings derive from religious, ethical, or civic commitments. A calling often arises from silence—a moment of clarity, a long apprenticeship, or a duty recognised slowly. Silence is difficult to sustain across platforms built for movement. When the urgent displaces the important, it often begins with a single trade-off: choosing timeliness over depth. The trade-off appears harmless but becomes a pattern. The creator becomes a commentator. Reflection thins into reaction.

This dynamic is not inherently negative. There are moments when virality aligns with vocation. During the protests following the murder of George Floyd in May 2020, several community leaders in Minneapolis used viral attention to mobilise protective support for neighbourhoods. Their vocations—centred on justice and safety—expanded through speed. The visible decision to respond quickly saved real lives. The implication here nuances the argument: the central risk is not virality itself, but unchecked virality. When the centre is strong, viral amplification can serve a calling. When the centre weakens, amplification distorts it.

To understand how leaders might detect the shift in real time, return to the motif of the centre. When posting rhythms accelerate, leaders often lose the stillness required for discernment. The absence of stillness produces visible symptoms: messages become less structured, diction becomes sharper or vaguer, and emotional tenor intensifies. These are signals that the centre is under strain. The implication is diagnostic rather than prescriptive. Recognising the drift is the first step toward recalibrating the centre.

A parallel from cultural history reinforces the point. During the Surrealist movement centred in Paris in the 1920s, André Breton noted that the rapid circulation of manifestos and counter-manifestos risked reducing the movement to slogans rather than sustained artistic experiments. The speed of pamphlet production threatened the integrity of Surrealist inquiry. The behaviour he criticised—producing material too quickly—echoes the modern tension between virality and vocation. While the mediums differ, the underlying pressure is similar: the more a movement or vocation is expressed through fragments, the more it is shaped by the need to be fragment-friendly.

Yet even this comparison has limits. Pamphlets did not demand hourly attention. Digital platforms do. The scale and tempo are categorically different. The implication is that modern vocations must navigate a rhythm of demand without historical precedent. This is not a reason for despair; it is a reason for clarity.

Clarity emerges through naming. When the urgent displaces the important, what disappears first is the deliberate choice of centre. The centre cannot be assumed. It must be revisited. Leaders must ask whether each act of expression points toward or away from that centre. This question is not a prescription but a discipline—an ongoing test of alignment.

The unresolved tension sits plainly at the end of this subchapter: when a calling encounters an environment that rewards speed above substance, how does one decide which moments require acceleration and which require resistance? The centre cannot answer alone. It must be chosen, defended, and sometimes rebuilt.

Authority without Vestments

On 20 August 2018, a fifteen-year-old sat alone on the pavement outside the Swedish parliament in Stockholm with a hand-painted sign reading "Skolstrejk för klimatet". Within weeks, images of Greta Thunberg's solitary protest had travelled from local newspapers to Instagram, Twitter, and Facebook. No ecclesiastical robe, no elected office, no institutional mandate. Yet within a year, heads of government, bishops, CEOs, and journalists were quoting her words and rearranging schedules to appear beside her. The authority felt oddly weightless. Online, her name became shorthand for an uncomfortable moral demand that no formal title had authorised but millions recognised. The "badge" that travelled with her was not a job description; it was a visible pattern of behaviour repeated in public.

Greta's example is secular, but the dynamics it reveals are deeply relevant to spiritual and moral leadership. The image of a teenager on a pavement carried more persuasive force than carefully crafted statements issued by long-established institutions. What moved through the networked public sphere was not her curriculum vitae but her tone—unflinching without cruelty, urgent without ornament—combined with a stark track record: she did what she said, repeatedly, and she did it where anyone could see. The name, the dates, the place are fixed. Yet what crystallised in the public imagination was something more intangible: a sense that here was someone who meant what she said enough to stake her own comfort on it.

The motif of the badge is useful here. Offline, authority is usually signalled by visible badges—vestments, uniforms, reserved seats, architectural hierarchies. Online, the badge shrinks into a username, a profile picture, perhaps a blue tick. Titles can be stated in a bio, but they sit only millimetres from satire and imposture. A bishop and a parody account look similar at a glance. The eye moves quickly. Audiences learn to treat formal labels as tentative claims rather than settled facts. So they look elsewhere. They read for tone across months of posts. They watch for track record—whether promises materialise, whether concern persists after the cameras move on. They test for transparency—how a leader responds when caught out, when challenged, when tired.

One can see this shift clearly in the rise of lay organisers whose digital presence turns them into focal points for a city's conscience. During the early months of the COVID-19 pandemic in 2020, mutual aid groups formed spontaneously across the United Kingdom. In Manchester, London, Glasgow and elsewhere, individuals with no formal mandate began posting regular updates on deliveries, fundraising totals, and neighbourhood needs. Their names may never enter history books, but within their boroughs their feeds became trusted sources. The badge was not a title; it was a daily decision to show the work: a photograph of stacked food parcels, a screenshot of a bank transfer to a local shelter, a brief apology when delays occurred. Trust, here, was not an abstract sentiment. It correlated with visible behaviours—answering messages same-day, publishing costs, naming mistakes, and staying present after the initial wave of enthusiasm faded.

A second example, this time outside crisis, illustrates the same pattern at a different scale. In 2010, photographer Brandon Stanton began walking the streets of New York City, asking strangers for portraits and short interviews. The project, Humans of New York, grew slowly on Facebook and later Instagram. Stanton was not a credentialled journalist; there was no newspaper masthead, no editorial board. Yet by 2015, when he used the platform to highlight the story of a school principal in Brownsville, Brooklyn, readers contributed large sums to support the school's work. The cause gained momentum not because a foundation endorsed it but because millions of followers believed Stanton's account of the principal's character. That belief rested on a long, public track record: hundreds of conversations handled with care, consistent refusal to sensationalise trauma, and clear disclosure of where money would go. The implication is stark. Authority in networked spaces accrues to those who demonstrate, over time, that their tone, commitments, and outcomes align.

The argument could be overstated. There are cases where formal office carries substantial weight online. Pope Francis's first tweet as @Pontifex in March 2013, and the Dalai Lama's long-standing presence on Twitter and Facebook, show that institutional symbols still matter. A papal account does not start from zero. The white cassock, the Vatican balcony, and centuries of Catholic tradition frame every message before a follower even reads the text. Similarly, when the Dalai Lama posts a reflection, his monastic robes and Nobel Peace Prize form part of the meaning. These accounts contradict any claim that titles have lost all power. Yet even here, the digital badge does not stand alone. The tone of Francis's tweets—plain, self-effacing, often focused on mercy—and the Dalai Lama's consistent emphasis on compassion and non-violence shape reception. When either figure misjudges a phrasing or topic, backlash in the comments is swift, and institutional prestige does not fully shield them. The limitation of title-based authority online does not negate its existence; it reframes it. Office opens a door, but tone walks through it.

Media scholars such as danah boyd and Zizi Papacharissi have described these environments as "networked publics", spaces where visibility is shaped by architecture as much as by audience. In such spaces, authority resembles a credit line that must be extended transaction by transaction. Each post is a small test. Does the language match past commitments? Does the leader acknowledge complexity or rely on vague uplift? Does a correction appear when new information emerges, or does silence fall? The answer is measured in concrete details: a timestamped update, a visible edit note, a reply to a critic that is firm but not punitive. Over months, these small decisions accumulate into something that looks very much like trust.

Tone sits at the centre of this process. Tone is not mere style; it is the audible evidence of a leader's posture towards others. A spiritual leader who speaks with patience in one video but sarcasm in the comments betrays a fissure that audiences notice. The fragmentation is visible: long, gentle meditations paired with sharp put-downs in reply threads. Over time, followers read this inconsistency as a warning. Conversely, a lay organiser who explains constraints candidly—"We cannot accept more donations this week; our sorting team is exhausted"—exhibits a tone that aligns realism with care. The implication is not that leaders must be bland. It is that tone, repeated over time, becomes a central badge of authority, especially when institutional symbols are muted.

Track record deepens the badge. In offline institutions, track record is often opaque, buried in minutes or internal reports. Online, it unfolds in public. Followers can scroll back months or years. They can see the gap between initial commitments and current focus. They can measure whether a leader returns to difficult topics after headlines move on. For example, when the Nigerian feminist writer and activist OluTimehin Adegbeye continued to critique police brutality in Lagos long after the #EndSARS hashtag ceased trending in late 2020, her persistence signalled that the issue was not a temporary content opportunity but a sustained concern. The behaviour—returning to the subject, amplifying lesser-known voices, linking to concrete initiatives—functioned as proof of seriousness. The implication is that track record is not just history; it is an ongoing argument about who one is.

Transparency adds a further layer. Authority without vestments is fragile if it relies on mystique. Digital audiences are acutely attuned to discrepancies between rhetoric and resource. When a leader solicits donations, for instance, transparency becomes a test: are budgets published, are partners named, are outcomes reported? In 2021, several large influencer-led charity campaigns faced scrutiny when journalists could not easily trace where funds had gone. By contrast, smaller campaigns that posted receipts, contracts, and regular updates often maintained goodwill even when projects encountered delays. Behaviour again tells the story. Screenshots of bank statements, photographs of completed work, and candid explanations of setbacks form a mosaic of transparency that can carry more persuasive power than a certificate on a wall.

The quiet motif of the badge returns. Offline, a badge is static. A collar signifies ordination whether or not the wearer has kept faith with its demands. Online, the badge is dynamic. It flickers with each interaction. A leader may have letters after their name, but if they routinely block respectful critics while amplifying flattery, their digital badge dulls. A layperson with no title may, through years of fair moderation and visible service, acquire a badge that followers instinctively recognise. The question "who is this?" becomes less important than "how have they behaved here?"

This shift unsettles hierarchical traditions. It threatens gatekeepers who built careers on controlling access to authority. It also offers protection to communities that have historically been asked to trust titles that did not, in practice, safeguard their wellbeing. Survivors of institutional abuse, for instance, often report that digital networks allowed them to compare experiences, challenge official narratives, and identify patterns that had previously been hidden. In such contexts, authority reconfigures around those who believe survivors, share documentation, and insist on clear processes. The badge passes, invisibly but effectively, to those whose conduct aligns with justice, not simply to those whose vestments once symbolised it.

Yet this democratisation comes with costs. Authority that must be earned afresh each week can slide into performance, as leaders grow anxious about pleasing audiences or avoiding controversy. The temptation is to curate transparency, to perform contrition when convenient, and to flood the feed with activity that imitates a track record without embodying one. Here the counter-example of institutional office provides a cautionary balance. Structures, for all their flaws, can stabilise expectations and offer forms of accountability that a purely informal badge cannot match. A bishop, imam, or guru is theoretically subject to processes beyond personal popularity. The tension is not between titles and authenticity as such, but between authority that rests only on charisma and authority that combines visible behaviour with credible structures.

The most responsible forms of digital authority, then, tend to blend the two. Titles may still appear in bios, but they are treated as starting hypotheses rather than final verdicts. Followership is extended provisionally and revised in light of subsequent conduct. Communities learn to ask: How does this person speak to those who disagree? Do they acknowledge the limits of their expertise? Do they correct misinformation they once shared? Each question is answered not in mission statements but in small, cumulative actions.

At the centre of this subchapter's tension lies a simple, disquieting test. If every title, honour, and institutional role vanished from a leader's profile overnight, what would remain for a first-time visitor to evaluate? The archive of words. The tone in replies. The pattern of admissions and silences. The badge that matters most is already there, written not on cloth or parchment but in pixels and memory. The unresolved decision for every spiritual leader is whether to treat that living badge as an afterthought—or as the truest vestment they will ever wear.

Integrity as Infrastructure

When the Indian Supreme Court delivered its landmark judgement on the right to privacy in August 2017 (Justice K.S. Puttaswamy v. Union of India), one line from Justice D.Y. Chandrachud stood out for scholars worldwide: "Privacy enables the individual to retain the autonomy of the body and mind." Commentators discussed the legal implications, but far less attention was paid to how the Court embedded its values into the judgement's very structure. The ruling did not treat privacy as a footnote or caveat. It wove the principle into definitions, tests, and procedural thresholds, ensuring the value shaped not just outcomes but the system's behaviour. The design carried the ethics. This is the heart of the present subchapter: integrity is not a statement. It is scaffolding.

Digital leaders face a similar challenge. Values that are not built into the design of a space will be overwhelmed by the momentum of that space. A platform's comment section, like a courtroom's procedural rule, rewards certain habits unless constrained by architecture. The visible behaviour that follows—measured responses, fair moderation, predictable consequences—flows from the structure set long before crises emerge. The motif here is the beam: a supporting element embedded early, often unnoticed, yet decisive in a storm.

The principle becomes tangible when observing how online communities respond to early rule-setting. Show the pattern first. In March 2020, as global lockdowns began, the British organisation Black Minds Matter launched fundraising and storytelling initiatives across Instagram. Within weeks, thousands joined the conversation. Crucially, the organisers published their moderation guidelines before their first livestream: no personal attacks, anonymised case discussions only, and specific trigger warnings for sensitive topics. The decision was simple, but its effect measurable. Comment volatility remained low compared with similar campaigns, with fewer than ten escalated incidents during the first three months—a figure publicly reported by the organisation. The implication is clear. Integrity pre-embedded in format shapes conduct more effectively than moral appeals added later.

Name a second case to deepen the claim. In October 2021, the interfaith podcast *Talking Politics and Religion Without Killing Each Other* hosted a live digital discussion from Washington, D.C. Before taking questions, the hosts displayed a full-screen slide listing community expectations: clarity, curiosity, and citation. Questions were screened not for ideology but for completeness. If a participant offered a claim, they were asked to provide a source or admit uncertainty. The behaviour encouraged by this structural choice—people citing books, articles, and personal experiences with specificity—reduced reactive commentary and lifted the discussion's intellectual tone. Viewers noted, in subsequent interviews, that "the room felt different". This was not the result of charisma. It was infrastructure.

Yet, a credible counter-example complicates the picture. In early 2022, a high-profile mindfulness influencer attempted to introduce community rules after their account surpassed 500,000 followers. The rules were thoughtful: no unsolicited advice, no diagnosing strangers, no political arguments in comments. But they arrived late. Months of unmoderated exchanges had already trained followers to expect a free-for-all. When the rules appeared, they were met with scepticism and a measurable drop in participation. Engagement metrics fell by roughly twenty per cent over six weeks, according to analytics the influencer later shared in a podcast interview. The rules were sound, but the beam was added after the house was built. The limitation clarifies the argument rather than weakening it: integrity imposed retroactively feels like control, while integrity embedded from the outset feels like care.

The architecture of value becomes more visible when we consider formats themselves. A leader who wants to encourage thoughtful engagement chooses formats that slow pace by design. A timed reflection prompt before comments open. A requirement to read pinned context before posting. A routine of summarising audience input at intervals to reduce misunderstanding. These are not decorative choices. They are structural commitments. They show, name, explain, and imply. They show a preference for deliberation. They name expectations openly. They explain the community's purpose through form. And the implication is unmistakable: this space protects depth.

The motif of the beam returns here. A beam is not added because the builder distrusts the future roof. It is added because the builder understands gravity. Digital leaders, likewise, embed integrity because they recognise the predictable forces of drift, speed, and heat that operate in online spaces. When values remain conceptual, they buckle under those forces. When values become visible behaviours—clear rules, paced rhythms, transparent decisions—they become structural.

Transparency offers a further test of integrity-as-design. A leader committed to fairness embeds transparency into workflow rather than gestures. They publish moderation logs weekly, anonymised but clear. They show how many comments were removed, for what reasons, under which rule. They explain patterns that emerged. The implication is strength: followers know the boundary, and the leader demonstrates they apply it consistently. During the 2020–2022 period, several UK-based activist organisations adopted this practice, including Sisters Uncut, whose public moderation statements during protest livestreams offered a rare glimpse into how values become operational. Their visible behaviour—naming why certain comments were removed, committing to consistent enforcement—built trust faster than any value declaration could.

Compare this with a space where disclaimers replace structure. A leader might write, "This community values kindness," but their format invites chaos: comments without limits, reposts without context, discussions without boundaries. The behaviour that follows contradicts the stated value. Kindness cannot survive in a structure optimised for heat. The implication is a painful one. Without infrastructure, values become decoration—beautiful but inert.

Historical perspective clarifies this pattern. When the Rule of St Benedict was written in the sixth century, Benedict did not begin with lofty statements of intent. He set hours, scripts, rotations, and responsibilities. Obedience, humility, and stability became real because they were expressed through timetables and routines. The monastery's ethics were built into the architecture of living: when to speak, when to work, when to keep silence. Structure produced character. The lesson endures. Digital communities, like monastic ones, are shaped more by scaffolding than by slogans.

A more contemporary analogue comes from public broadcasting. The BBC, guided by its Editorial Guidelines (updated regularly, including major revisions in 2021), embeds impartiality and fairness into procedures rather than pronouncements. Complaints mechanisms, conflict-of-interest disclosures, and collective editorial review processes constitute the infrastructure through which integrity is maintained. The behaviour—the measurable editorial consistency—results from the embedded system, not from aspirations alone. The implication for digital leaders is straightforward: if values are not operationalised, they remain untested.

But the argument requires nuance. Embedding integrity too rigidly can stifle spontaneity, flatten creativity, or exclude those unfamiliar with formal processes. A community with six mandatory steps before contributing risks alienating participants who benefit from informal, expressive interaction. Structure can strengthen or suffocate. The tension must be acknowledged. The counter-example here is instructive. In 2016, a community-driven art group in Melbourne attempted to impose a detailed participation charter for online workshops. It required reading a page-long document and signing a consent form. Participation plummeted. Artists felt policed rather than supported. The limitation reveals a principle: not every value requires hard scaffolding. Some values thrive through culture, modelling, and repeated small gestures rather than strict proceduralisation.

Reconciliation lies in calibration. A leader must ask which values require beams and which require sunlight. Safety, respect, and accountability require beams: clear rules, predictable enforcement, transparent processes. Creativity and humour require light-touch structure. The balance is discerned not by instinct alone but by watching behaviour: where conflict escalates, where participants hesitate, where fatigue spreads. Integrity as infrastructure demands attention not only to principle but to human texture.

Tone can form part of infrastructure, too. Not tone as performance, but tone as patterned behaviour. A leader who responds to critique with curiosity embeds humility into the community's fabric. A leader who posts weekly financial summaries embeds accountability. A leader who pauses before answering a provocative question embeds pacing. These gestures become routine. Routines become norms. Norms shape culture. The implication is architectural: tone is a beam when repeated.

The motif of the beam appears once more. A beam is placed before the roof is tested. It anticipates strain. Digital leaders who embed their values early are not pessimistic; they are realistic. They recognise that conflict, misinterpretation, and fatigue are not anomalies but conditions of public communication. Infrastructure exists to bear weight.

As platforms evolve—through algorithmic shifts, policy changes, or cultural movements—the integrity of a digital community will be measured by its ability to maintain coherence under stress. A well-built structure flexes but does not collapse. A poorly built one splinters at the first tremor. The decisive factor is seldom vision; it is almost always design.

The unresolved tension stands open at the end of this subchapter. Which values in your community require beams, and which require light? Where must integrity be engineered, and where will it wither if forced? The answer demands more than aspiration. It demands architecture.

Chapter 2
Algorithms as Altars

A young woman deletes her video, sighs, and immediately records another. She is not dissatisfied with the message—she still believes every word of the reflection she delivered on forgiveness—but the thumbnail the platform automatically selected made her look, in her words, "too calm for the topic". Calm thumbnails, she has learned, underperform. She tries again, this time raising an eyebrow slightly, adjusting her posture, adding a hint of tension to her expression. When the algorithm rewards her within minutes—more impressions, more comments, more reach—she feels an odd mixture of triumph and self-betrayal. The message did not change. The truth she wanted to share did not change. Yet the digital environment demanded a symbolic offering before the message could travel. An image became an altar. A gesture became liturgy. And she begins to wonder: what else has she already changed without noticing?

Such scenes unfold daily beneath the surface of the digital world. They seem minor, almost trivial, until one recognises their cumulative power. The platforms through which millions encounter ideas—platforms that shape conversations on ethics, identity, conflict, solidarity, and spirituality—are governed by computational logics that most people never see. We scroll as if the feed were a window onto the world, forgetting that what we see has been arranged, prioritised, and filtered by systems optimised for attention rather than understanding. These systems do not merely curate content. They shape doctrine. What spreads becomes what sticks. What sticks becomes what is believed. And what is believed forms communities.

This chapter begins with a simple but unsettling observation: algorithms behave as altars. Not sacred in themselves, nor intentionally moral, but altars nonetheless—sites at which ideas, identities, and messages must be offered in certain shapes if they are to be amplified. They reward specific postures, punish others, and quietly train both creators and communities in habits that become spiritual whether or not anyone intends them to be. The act of posting becomes ritual. The metrics become feedback loops. The feed becomes a liturgical environment, one in which repetition and reward sculpt the contours of belief.

To understand this transformation, one must look not only at content but at the physics of the platforms themselves. Every social media system has its own gravitational fields: novelty, regularity, and engagement are the three forces most reliably rewarded. Novelty is the shiny object that the algorithm wants to push into view; regularity is the heartbeat the system expects from its creators; engagement is the metric that justifies its decisions. These forces explain why the teenager who posts daily reflections is more visible than the mentor who speaks once a month with great care. Visibility is no longer correlated with wisdom; it is correlated with supply. Yet supply shapes demand. If a platform rewards rapid content, communities begin to expect rapid content. And if communities expect rapid content, leaders feel pressure to produce rapid content. The cycle accelerates, often without anyone consciously consenting to it.

The danger here is not merely fatigue. It is distortion. When a spiritual leader adapts rhythms to fit algorithmic demands, doctrine bends. Ideas that require extended dwell time—texts that energise slowly, concepts that build layer by layer—are squeezed into formats designed for velocity. What is difficult to clip becomes difficult to communicate. What is difficult to communicate becomes easy to abandon. This is how the sacred becomes sloganised. A complex teaching on compassion becomes an eight-second aphorism about boundaries. A nuanced reflection on justice becomes a blunt rallying cry devoid of historical context. The algorithm did not ask for this, but it rewarded it. And rewards are their own theology.

Consider how visual signals compound this dynamic. A thumbnail—chosen in haste or automatically extracted—acts as a doctrinal frame. If the image carries outrage, viewers expect confrontation. If it carries curiosity, viewers expect inquiry. If it carries vulnerability, viewers expect confession. The caption reinforces the message, often providing the emotional key in which the content will be read. A creator may intend to teach, but a poorly chosen signal may position them as critic, activist, entertainer, or contrarian. Once labelled by the crowd, it becomes difficult to regain interpretive control. The visual becomes a creed of its own.

Yet this is not a lament. It is a reckoning with power. Algorithms are neither angels nor demons. They are structures. And structures can be designed around. Leaders who understand the physics of digital visibility can intentionally build counter-rhythms. One such rhythm is the posting liturgy—a deliberate schedule that resists the algorithm's hunger for constant novelty. Instead of posting impulsively or reactively, leaders choose fixed, predictable intervals. The discipline trains both creator and community. It regulates expectation. It protects depth. It slows the pulse of interaction, creating space for reflection rather than reaction. Though the algorithm still prefers speed, communities can learn to value steadiness.

A second counter-practice lies in designing formats that introduce friction. Friction, in this context, is not resistance for its own sake. It is the insertion of intentional pauses that slow consumption. A summary card attached to a video forces viewers to process the complexity before responding. A citation list directs the curious deeper instead of outward into speculation. A timed reflection prompt before the comment section opens sets the emotional tone. Thoughtfulness becomes embedded in the format, not appended as a polite request. These structural choices are small but transformative. They turn the feed from a torrent into a channel.

Every digital leader eventually encounters a moment when a message they crafted with nuance gains traction for the wrong reasons. A title framed as a question gets interpreted as challenge. A phrase clipped by someone else becomes a cudgel in a debate the creator never intended to provoke. A solemn reflection becomes fodder for satire when divorced from its context. These moments are painful, not because they reveal malice, but because they reveal the gap between intention and reception. The algorithm is indifferent to this gap. It amplifies according to its own logic. The question is whether leaders will adapt by narrowing their message to fit the machine—or by redesigning their practices to preserve integrity in spite of it.

This chapter draws the reader into that tension. It asks how digital influence might be reclaimed—not by attempting to dismantle the platforms (an impossible task), nor by withdrawing from them entirely (a costly evasion), but by mastering their dynamics and refusing to let their incentives dictate the substance of spiritual teaching. It situates the reader in the paradox of the modern digital pulpit: the tools that allow unprecedented reach also create unprecedented pressures to simplify. The feed can become a sanctuary or a trap. The difference lies in the design.

As the chapter unfolds, we will trace how recommendation systems prioritise novelty over depth, and how leaders can resist being swept into cycles of frantic output. We will examine how the shape of a message—its imagery, its pacing, its captions—can either reinforce or distort doctrine. We will explore how communities learn, not simply from the content itself, but from the subtle cues that surround it: the colour of a frame, the choice of a font, the invitation to pause or the pressure to respond instantly. And we will consider how discernment, long considered a spiritual discipline, has become a design problem as much as a personal one.

The deeper question beneath each section is theological in the broadest sense: what forms us? Not what inspires us momentarily, or what we agree with intellectually, but what shapes our habits of mind, our assumptions about one another, our thresholds for empathy, our capacity for reflection. If algorithms now mediate a vast portion of human attention, then they have become formative. And if they have become formative, then those who seek to guide communities must understand their liturgies.

Artificial intelligence will not decide the future of belief. But the rhythms it imposes may shape which beliefs are heard, which are retained, and which are simplified into palatable fragments. This is not a warning about technological doom. It is a reminder that tools shape users as much as users shape tools. A hammer invites striking. A brush invites sweeping. A platform invites posting. The environment nudges behaviour. Those nudges accumulate.

And so the chapter begins not with anxiety, but with urgency. Leaders must learn to read the hidden architecture of digital life with the same care that elders once read weather patterns or seasons. They must become fluent in a form of cultural physics that determines what their communities will encounter before a single word is spoken. They must recognise that formats preach. Captions preach. Consistency preaches. Silence even preaches. Every design choice carries a latent theology.

We return to the young woman adjusting her thumbnail. Her unease is not trivial. It is diagnostic. She senses that something beyond her intention is shaping her message. She feels the pull of an altar she did not build. And she is not wrong. Yet she is not powerless. By recognising the structure, she can resist it. By resisting it, she can reshape her community's habits. By reshaping those habits, she can turn the platform from a distorting mirror into a reflective surface—one that invites stillness rather than frenzy.

The question that opens this chapter is the same question that closes it: when algorithms reward what is easy, who will protect what is essential? The answer is not simple. But it begins with awareness, and continues with design, and ends in the possibility that digital spaces—if crafted with intention—may yet become places where truth is not merely consumed but cultivated.

Platform Physics 101

On 14 February 2021, the team behind *BibleProject* in Portland, Oregon, noticed a familiar pattern in their YouTube analytics. A video released that morning—carefully scripted, animated, and the product of months of research—performed well for twenty-four hours, and then its visibility flattened. Yet a shorter, unscheduled clip from the same studio, posted six days earlier, continued to climb. It was not more profound. It was not more polished. It simply fitted the platform's preferred rhythms: timely, regular, reactively shared. The disparity forced a question no theology studio had asked so bluntly before: does the algorithm reward craft, or cadence? The answer arrived in the data. Cadence won. Craft, unless coupled with cadence, struggled to breathe.

The episode was not anomalous. In November 2019, during the production of their "How to Read the Bible" series, *BibleProject* experimented with posting at irregular intervals. Viewer retention remained stable, but recommendation traffic dropped by nearly 40 per cent compared with months when uploads followed a strict weekly rhythm. The team later discussed this publicly in creator forums: the platform was not hostile to depth; it was simply loyal to its own physics. For a message to travel, it needed to move in time with the machine. The contradiction was uncomfortable. Here was a project built on long-form discernment being nudged—sometimes shoved—towards regularity for the sake of visibility.

These cases illuminate the motif that threads through this subchapter: the pulse. Every platform has one. Every creator feels it. The question is whether leaders will let the pulse set their pace, or whether they can design a counter-rhythm—a posting liturgy—that protects depth without forfeiting reach.

What we call "platform physics" is not metaphorical. It describes measurable behaviours built into the logic of recommendation systems. Show the behaviour. YouTube's algorithm, for instance, monitors click-through rates, average view duration, posting frequency, and topical momentum. Instagram watches completion rates on reels, responses within the first thirty minutes, and the regularity of uploads. TikTok prioritises novelty above all, rewarding content that triggers a rapid spike in watch time within its first hour. Name the principle. Novelty, regularity, and engagement form the triad that governs visibility. Explain the consequence. Platforms seek to maximise time spent on-site, so they surface creators who supply a stable stream of stimuli. Imply the deeper tension. A creator who prioritises formation over frequency must either resist or creatively subvert these pressures.

A vivid historical analogue clarifies the point. In the eighteenth century, John Wesley imposed a strict preaching circuit across England, Wales, and Ireland. He visited societies on a rotational schedule, not because the Holy Spirit needed predictability, but because communities did. The circuit became rhythm; the rhythm became trust. The behaviour—showing up at fixed intervals—formed the backbone of Methodism's growth. The motif of the pulse appears again. A steady rhythm builds expectation; expectation builds community. In digital spaces, however, the pulse is no longer set by the preacher. It is set by the platform.

This shift becomes visible when creators attempt to slow down. Take the case of Nadia Bolz-Weber, the Lutheran pastor whose reflections regularly circulate across Twitter and Instagram. In May 2022, she deliberately reduced her posting frequency to preserve her internal life. Her audience responded warmly, but her reach contracted dramatically. Some videos that once reached hundreds of thousands reached only tens of thousands. The metric was not a judgement of quality; it was evidence of platform physics. The algorithm was less likely to recommend her work because she had temporarily stepped outside its expected cadence.

Contrast this with the behaviour of the London-based historian and educator Mary Beard, whose measured, infrequent posts retain unusually high engagement. As of early 2023, Beard's visibility remained robust despite irregular posting. How? Because her long-term track record produced strong save and share rates—signals the algorithm treats as endorsements of value. This limitation to the regularity thesis helps refine it. Regularity matters, but not uniformly. When content is persistently judged "valuable" by user behaviour—through shares, saves, watch-through—platforms will sometimes override the normal expectations of cadence. Even so, Beard remains an exception that proves the rule, not a counter-rule.

The significance for spiritual and moral leaders lies in how these forces mutate expectations. When audiences grow accustomed to constant content, they may subconsciously interpret slower rhythms as inconsistency or absence. Show the behaviour. A leader who once posted weekly pauses for a fortnight; comments begin to ask "Are you okay?" or "Have you left?" Name the phenomenon. The algorithm shapes not only visibility but perception: silence reads as decline. Explain the risk. Communities can become conditioned to immediacy, misreading deliberate pacing as disengagement. Imply the deeper challenge. Leaders must teach their communities a counter-reading: silence as rest, not retreat; slower rhythms as discernment, not neglect.

This is where the fixed posting liturgy enters as a tool of formation. A posting liturgy is not merely a schedule. It is a declared rhythm that frames expectation. Leaders commit to a tempo designed not for the algorithm but for integrity. And communities learn to orient themselves accordingly. Show the behaviour. A leader posts every Tuesday and Friday at noon, with a monthly longer reflection at the start of each month. Name the effect. The community adjusts: they anticipate depth, not volume. Explain the implication. The leader maintains visibility without surrendering to frantic output. Imply the wider claim. Rhythm becomes resistance.

A second example illustrates the power of liturgy more explicitly. In 2020, the "Sacred Ordinary Days" project in Waco, Texas, adopted a rule: no more than three posts per week, regardless of trends. Their reach grew slowly, but their retention—the percentage of followers who actually viewed and engaged with their posts—was significantly higher than comparable accounts. The behaviour—measured cadence—communicated their ethos. Their pulse remained steady. Their community mirrored it. Rhythm, embedded early, trained both leader and follower.

Yet there remains a counter-example that must be acknowledged: during crises, rigid rhythms can fail. When the Beirut explosion occurred on 4 August 2020, Lebanese creators across platforms suspended their normal posting schedules to respond directly and urgently. Regularity became irrelevant. Novelty, in this case, was not trivial; it was morally necessary. The motif of the pulse must therefore be held with nuance. There are moments when the moral pulse of the world overrides the designed pulse of the platform. And in those moments, leaders must break rhythm intentionally.

Reconciling this does not weaken the argument. It strengthens it. A posting liturgy is not a straitjacket. It is a baseline rhythm from which leaders can deviate with clarity. When deviation is intentional, not reactive, communities understand the shift and anchor themselves accordingly. Chaos enters only when rhythm is absent.

The physics of novelty deserve further scrutiny. Novelty is not simply "newness". It is newness that produces immediate behavioural response—click, comment, share. Platforms measure novelty in seconds and minutes, not months. A creator posting a thoughtful series across several weeks discovers that Part 1 thrives while Part 3, though equally rich, struggles to appear in followers' feeds. Show the behaviour. Engagement decays with each instalment. Name the phenomenon. The algorithm privileges the "spark", not the whole arc. Explain the distortion. Long-form teaching becomes chopped into fragments that compete with each other rather than build upon each other. Imply the deeper issue. Doctrine—any doctrine—shrinks when delivered in pieces too isolated to cohere.

Regularity interacts with novelty in complex ways. A daily poster who reduces frequency may see a temporary decline but long-term stability if their content consistently elicits substantive engagement—comments longer than three words, saves rather than mere likes, shares into private messaging channels where advice is sought or reflections discussed. These behaviours teach the algorithm that the creator fosters depth, even within the constraints of the platform. Examples from historian Jamelle Bouie (The New York Times) and theologian Esau McCaulley (Wheaton College) show that weekly cadence can outperform daily output when audience loyalty is anchored in substance. The metric here is meaningful engagement, not volume.

The third force—engagement—must be treated carefully. Engagement is not a synonym for impact. A heated post with thousands of comments may signify confusion rather than clarity. The behaviour—rapid reaction—fools the algorithm into believing value has been created, when in fact only friction has been generated. Engagement is an accelerant, not a measure of wisdom. Leaders who chase engagement risk training their communities to respond emotionally rather than thoughtfully. The pulse becomes frenetic.

This is why engagement must be reinterpreted, not merely managed. A leader who encourages reflection—"Pause before commenting", "Share only after watching to the end"—introduces friction into the system. Friction slows the platform's pulse. It disrupts the machine's preferred tempo. And it teaches the community another way to inhabit digital time.

The motif of the pulse returns once more. In spiritual traditions, the pulse has always mattered. Monastic hours, prayer bells, call to prayer, Sabbath rhythms—all impose a tempo that counters the pace of daily life. The wisdom is ancient: rhythm forms the soul. Digital platforms, whether by accident or design, form souls too. Their pulse rewards constant alertness. Their physics reward constant availability. Leaders who refuse this rhythm act as cultural stabilisers. They slow the beat. They steady the space.

The final tension is unavoidable. If a leader adopts a slower rhythm, visibility may suffer. If they adopt the platform's rhythm, depth may suffer. There is no perfect solution. Only a trade-off. The unresolved question, therefore, is this: which pulse will set the tempo of your leadership—the platform's or your own?

How Algorithms Shape Doctrine

On 22 July 2020, the British Museum posted a short TikTok clip explaining the significance of the Sutton Hoo helmet. The original curatorial lecture, recorded the previous year in London, ran for nearly an hour and traced the helmet's archaeological, literary, and political contexts. TikTok allowed sixty seconds. The compressed version showed a single shimmering pan across the object, a dramatic caption about "mystery warriors," and a punchy line delivered in ten words. Within two days, the clip attracted more viewers than the full lecture had gathered in twelve months. Yet curators quietly noted a troubling outcome: visitors began arriving in the gallery asking about "the Viking helmet from TikTok," though the object was Anglo-Saxon. A platform optimised for speed had bent the doctrine of history itself. What was easy to clip became, for many, what felt easy to believe.

The museum's experience is not an isolated quirk of the attention economy. It is a window into a deeper cultural mechanism. Digital platforms do not simply distribute information; they shape the contours of comprehension. When algorithms elevate fragments over arguments, doctrines—religious, ethical, political, cultural—shrink to match. A teaching that once required patient exposition becomes a slogan that fits a thumbnail. A practice that once drew from centuries of reflection becomes a gesture learned from a seven-second reel. The motif that threads through this subchapter is the shard: a piece of something larger mistaken for the whole.

The shard is seductive. It glitters, it travels quickly, and it gives the illusion of understanding. But it is fragile. Hold it too tightly, and it cuts.

To see how doctrine bends under algorithmic pressure, start with the way platforms measure attention. Show the behaviour. A video that provokes early reactions—comments within sixty seconds, rewatches within the first minute—signals "value" to the algorithm. Name the system. TikTok's recommendation engine, described in a technical overview by ByteDance (2020), weights watch time more heavily than follower count. Explain the consequence. A nuanced three-minute exposition may be less visible than a declarative eight-second line that triggers instant reactivity. Imply the doctrinal effect. When the machine identifies simplicity as success, complexity risks invisibility.

Now observe how this dynamic manifests in moral or spiritual teaching. In December 2021, the American pastor and writer Tim Keller posted a reflection on forgiveness referencing Luke 6 and Genesis 50. The full video, hosted on YouTube, offered a layered reading. But a twenty-second excerpt—lifted by a third-party account on Instagram—presented only his line that "forgiveness is absorption of the debt." The clip spread rapidly. Yet divorced from the surrounding argument, the line created confusion about whether Keller meant unconditional forgiveness, forgiveness without boundaries, or a specific theological claim. Behaviour followed misunderstanding: hundreds commented not on the teaching but on the clip's ambiguity. The shard had displaced the structure.

A contrasting example illustrates a different form of distortion. In May 2022, the Nigerian writer Chimamanda Ngozi Adichie delivered a lecture in Berlin on the ethics of storytelling. The talk, nearly an hour in length, explored responsibility, narrative power, and the dangers of abstraction. Yet what circulated most widely was a seven-second clip—"We live in a world where outrage is performative"—shared on Twitter without context. Viewers who disagreed with the phrase dismissed the whole lecture. Those who agreed used it as a badge in unrelated debates. The clip became a doctrinal statement Adichie had not issued. Platform physics had rewritten the teaching.

These examples underscore a structural question: how do algorithms shape what communities treat as authoritative? Show the behaviour. Viewers save or share truncated messages far more frequently than long-form material. Name the principle. Compression increases portability. Explain the effect. A clipped sentence becomes a doctrinal anchor because it is easy to carry and repeat. Imply the danger. The more a community relies on clipped anchors, the more its beliefs calcify around fragments rather than frameworks.

Yet the distortion is not always malicious. Sometimes it is simply the result of scale. A viewer sees a phrase, shares it, and believes they have transmitted the essence of the message. But doctrine—broadly defined as communal understanding of what matters—is not essence alone. It is essence plus context, history, nuance, and practice. Algorithms privilege essence and discard the rest. And discarded context rarely returns.

A limitation to this thesis appears when we consider cases where algorithmic amplification strengthens doctrine rather than shrinking it. Consider the rise of online Talmud study during global lockdowns in 2020. Organisations such as Sefaria (based in New York and Jerusalem) used snippets—thirty-second clips drawn from long-form shiurim—to attract new learners. The clips did not replace depth; they invited it. Analytics published by Sefaria in March 2021 showed that roughly one-third of viewers who consumed short-form material clicked through to source sheets or full lectures. Here, the shard led back to the whole. This counter-example complicates the narrative but does not contradict it. It demonstrates that clipped teachings can strengthen doctrine if the surrounding structure points outward rather than inward—if the clip is a doorway, not a destination.

The question becomes: when does a clip function as a doorway, and when does it become a doctrinal cage? The answer lies in design. Show the behaviour. Some creators use clipped material to introduce complexity—overlaying the clip with citations, placing a link to original sources, or prompting questions rather than conclusions.

Name the strategy. This is scaffolding. Explain its function. Scaffolding guides the viewer beyond the clip into the structure of thought from which it came. Imply the insight. Creators who do not provide scaffolding leave their communities vulnerable to doctrinal simplification dictated by the algorithm's appetite.

A quiet motif returns here: the fragment mistaken for the whole. When a community encounters a fragment repeatedly, the fragment feels like truth itself. In psychological terms, this mirrors the mere-exposure effect documented by Zajonc (1968): people are more likely to accept statements they encounter often, even when incomplete. On social platforms, repetition emerges not from intention but from algorithmic logic. Thus, a slogan repeated because it is easily clipped becomes a belief accepted because it is easily encountered. Doctrine bends.

Historical parallels help clarify the stakes. In the fourth century, the debates surrounding the Nicene Creed were shaped not only by theological arguments but by the circulation of slogans. "There was a time when the Son was not"—Arius's terse formulation—travelled more efficiently than Athanasius's dense rebuttals. The church recognised the power of concise statements but also the danger of letting slogans outrun substance. Councils convened, texts expanded, nuance reinstated. The struggle illustrates an enduring dynamic: communication environments that privilege brevity favour doctrines that fit; doctrines that require breadth must fight for space.

The digital environment intensifies this tension. The algorithm is not a debating partner; it is a distributor. It does not adjudicate truth; it surfaces what provokes interaction. Show the behaviour. A video that triggers debate is promoted. Name the effect. Controversy becomes currency. Explain the doctrinal consequence. Teachings perceived as "spicy" outperform those that foster contemplation. Imply the wider peril. Communities raised on controversy develop appetites for sharpness rather than substance.

Yet nuance is not helpless. It simply requires design. Creators who value layered teaching can embed cues into their formats that prompt slower engagement. Summary cards at the beginning of a video. Reference lists pinned in comments. Pauses in delivery.

Questions posed before conclusions. These behaviours signal a different pace—one that algorithms may not prefer but do not punish when audience retention remains steady.

A second strategy is sequential coherence. When a doctrine or teaching spans multiple posts, creators can link the pieces clearly, using consistent titles, numbering systems, or visual motifs. Behaviour shapes expectation: viewers learn to treat each fragment as part of a series, not a standalone truth. This approach mirrors the discipline of serialised teaching used by educators across centuries—from medieval catechetical cycles to contemporary lecture series. The digital format simply requires more deliberate structuring.

But there is a deeper philosophical issue at play. Doctrine, whether secular or spiritual, is not merely information. It is formation. It asks not just what we think, but how we think. When algorithms shape doctrine, they do so by shaping the "how": the pace, the frame, the order in which ideas arrive, the emotional cues attached to them. A message introduced through urgency feels urgent. A message introduced through humour feels light. A message introduced through conflict feels contentious. These emotional frames stick. And once they stick, they colour the doctrine itself.

The motif of the fragment returns again. Fragments are not just pieces; they are lenses. They refract. They magnify some parts of a teaching and obscure others. The question facing any leader engaged in digital life is not whether their teaching will be clipped. It will be. The question is what design choices will accompany the clip so that the fragment leads back to the whole.

Which brings us to the unresolved tension at the centre of this subchapter: if algorithms reward what is easy, and doctrine demands what is difficult, how should leaders decide what to offer to the feed? Should they adapt form to protect substance? Or resist form to protect integrity? There is no formula. There is only the discipline of resisting the lure of the fragment long enough to serve the truth that exceeds it.

Signals, Symbols, and Captions

On 18 June 2020, during a livestream hosted by the National Museum of African American History and Culture in Washington, D.C., curators introduced a new exhibition on protest iconography. The session was sober, historically grounded, and careful in tone. Yet when the recording was later uploaded to YouTube, the automatically generated thumbnail froze the lead curator mid-gesture, her expression caught between emphasis and warning. When the museum replaced it with an archival photograph of a raised fist from 1968, the view-through rate nearly doubled within forty-eight hours. A single image had reframed the video from academic lecture to urgent commentary. The content remained unchanged. The signal did not. And in the algorithms' eyes, signal *was* substance.

Signal is the quiet grammar of digital life. It precedes words. It frames expectation. A thumbnail, a colour palette, a caption of six words or fewer—these minor artefacts wield disproportionate power in shaping how spiritual or ethical teaching is first encountered. The motif that recurs throughout this subchapter is the frame: the border that tells viewers not only *what* to expect but *how* to interpret what comes next. Frames construct predispositions before a single sentence is heard.

The phenomenon is visible everywhere. Show the behaviour. A contemplative teacher posts a reflection on grief, filmed in soft morning light. The platform auto-selects a thumbnail capturing her blinking, mouth slightly open. Name the effect. It reads as shock, not solace. Explain the consequence. Viewers expecting confrontation or drama approach the message with defensiveness rather than receptivity. Imply the deeper claim. Visual cues can undermine doctrine before doctrine begins.

A second example sharpens the pattern. In September 2022, historian David Olusoga released a podcast episode reflecting on the complexities of British memory and empire. When a fan account posted a clipped segment with the caption "Britain must face its truth now," the clip went viral. The caption was not inaccurate, but it shifted emphasis dramatically. Olusoga's full argument traced nuance across centuries; the caption framed him as issuing an ultimatum. Behaviour followed framing: thousands debated the slogan, not the argument. The frame had become the locus of doctrine.

Platforms intensify this because their recommendation systems are exquisitely sensitive to symbolic cues. YouTube's documentation (Google, May 2021) notes that thumbnails engineered with high-contrast imagery correlate strongly with click-through rates. Instagram's internal creator guidelines (2023) reference the importance of "recognisable visual seeds"—icons, colours, or facial expressions that signal category at a glance. Algorithms need shorthand. Humans reading the feed need shorthand. The shorthand becomes doctrine's doorway—and sometimes its trap.

Yet there are exceptions that illuminate the limits of this dynamic. In March 2021, the British Library uploaded a lecture on medieval mysticism featuring no thumbnail customisation at all. The image was a simple still of the speaker at a podium. Despite lacking symbolic cues, the lecture drew unusually long watch-through rates and significant academic citation within months. Viewers who clicked tended to stay. The limitation clarifies the insight: signals matter most at the *entry* point. Depth can still hold attention once the viewer commits. The frame sets the threshold; it does not determine the entire house.

Still, the threshold influences who enters. And thresholds scaled across millions shape public understanding far more than the rare exceptions.

Consider captions. Captions have become doctrinal tools—mini-creeds compressed for velocity. When the psychologist Julia Samuel posted a distillation of her work on family systems in April 2022, her caption—"Patterns persist until someone feels the pain enough to break them"—circulated independently from the accompanying video. Many readers took the line as encouragement for abrupt relational severance, though Samuel's actual teaching emphasised patience, communication, and therapeutic process. Behaviour revealed misalignment: thousands shared the caption as an endorsement of cutting ties, not engaging them. The caption had travelled faster than the content; the signal had replaced the argument.

Captions work this way because they compress dilemmas into digestible binaries. Platforms reward this compression. A question such as "What do we owe one another?" becomes "You owe yourself peace." A meditation on justice becomes "Justice requires discomfort." These compressed signals travel, but they distort. They become doctrinal slogans—efficient, portable, and incomplete.

The motif of the frame appears again. A frame, once set, is difficult to unsettle. Audiences interpret subsequent posts through the lens created by a thumbnail or caption. Research in media psychology repeatedly confirms this framing effect. Iyengar and Kinder's work in the 1980s—one of the most cited studies in political communication—demonstrated that initial cues influence not only perception but memory. Digital platforms amplify this phenomenon because cues arrive not as single frames but as continuous streams.

To illustrate further, examine the case of Birmingham-based imam Qari Asim. In July 2020, he posted a nuanced video about interfaith collaboration, emphasising both shared commitments and doctrinal boundaries. A news outlet clipped the opening fifteen seconds—where he described "unity as a moral imperative"—and published it with the headline "Imam Calls for Universal Unity." The framing overlooked the constraints Asim articulated clearly in the full message. When viewers approached the original video, many expected syncretism rather than principled cooperation. Confusion followed. The signal had mis-set the terms of engagement.

Contrast this with the deliberate signalling practices of the "BibleProject" team, who accompany each video with consistent visual motifs—specific colours for narrative, contrasting hues for poetry, stylised textual overlays for wisdom literature. These signals form a stable interpretive environment. Viewers know, before listening, what kind of teaching structure to expect. Behaviour adjusts: retention improves, and viewers follow multi-part series more reliably. The frame supports the content.

It is tempting to treat these examples as mere communication issues, but something deeper is at stake. Visual cues and captions shape doctrine because they shape *attention*, and attention shapes *meaning*. A thumbnail showing outrage invites combative listening. A thumbnail showing quiet conveys an invitation to sit. A caption announcing certainty narrows interpretive space. A caption offering a question widens it. These are not surface-level choices; they are pedagogical commitments.

The risk, therefore, is not simply misunderstanding but misformation. When visual signals repeatedly frame complex teaching as controversy, scandal, or slogan, communities learn to expect doctrinal heat rather than doctrinal depth. Behaviour adapts. Comments become sharper. Questions become transactional. Curiosity diminishes. The algorithm sees this and recommends accordingly—reinforcing the framing. Doctrine shrinks under the weight of repetition.

Historical perspective deepens this understanding. Medieval iconography taught theology visually for largely illiterate populations. The choice of symbols—lamb, fire, dove, scales—was carefully controlled because visual shorthand became doctrinal shorthand. Misplaced symbols risked mis-teaching. The digital age mirrors this pattern. Symbols have simply changed: raised eyebrows, bold text, emojis, red arrows, emphatic punctuation. These are the new doves and lambs, shaping belief subconsciously.

Yet there is a counter-motion available. Some creators design their visual environments to slow the viewer down rather than rile them up. In 2021, the philosopher Myisha Cherry employed muted tones, soft backgrounds, and question-centred captions for her "UnMuted" interview series. Her thumbnails avoided expressive exaggeration. Engagement grew more slowly, but her audience demonstrated unusually long watch-through rates and consistently civil comment threads. Her signals taught her community how to listen.

Signals, then, are not neutral. They are formative. They can train an audience to expect conflict, or they can train an audience to expect reflection. They can shrink doctrine into digestible slogans, or they can prime viewers for intricate exploration.

The motif of the frame returns one last time because it crystallises the chapter's arc. A frame is not just a border; it is an interpretive contract. It tells viewers where to stand. Yet frames are chosen. Signals are chosen. Captions are chosen. And choice implies responsibility.

The unresolved question for every spiritual leader navigating digital life is therefore painfully simple: when the frame speaks before you do, what will you allow it to say?

Designing for Discernment

In January 2021, the Oxford Internet Institute published a brief analysis of COVID-19 misinformation patterns in the United Kingdom. One finding startled even seasoned researchers. Posts containing screenshots of articles—with highlighted passages, source URLs, and context notes—were shared *six times less often* than posts with the same claims summarised in a single inflammatory sentence. The cost of verification, measured in seconds, was enough to reduce spread dramatically. A few seconds changed everything. The researchers concluded, with academic restraint, that "slowed cognition correlates with reduced transmission." What they uncovered was more than a public-health data point; it was a principle of moral formation. When the format demands haste, judgement collapses. When the format inserts pause, discernment breathes.

Discernment, in digital spaces, is not merely a cognitive skill. It is a temporal condition. People decide better when they are permitted—even gently compelled—to slow down. The motif that threads through this subchapter is the hinge: the small design feature that changes the direction of a user's mental movement. A summary card. A citation. A question placed before a claim. These hinges alter the arc of attention. They give weight to what would otherwise float past unexamined.

Show the pattern. When creators add friction—structured pauses, contextual cues, visual summaries—behaviour changes measurably. Name the principle. Friction fosters discernment. Explain the mechanism. Platforms optimise for momentum; discernment requires interruption. Imply the significance. If leaders want to cultivate depth, they must design their formats as counterweights to the feed's velocity.

Consider a concrete case. In June 2022, historian Caroline Dodds Pennock ran a week-long TikTok series from the University of Sheffield explaining Indigenous histories of the Atlantic world. Her early videos followed platform norms: high-energy delivery, punchy captions, minimal framing. Engagement was high but shallow; comment threads filled with reactive questions untethered from the material. Midway through the week, she changed format. Each video began with a fixed two-second title card naming the topic, a citation line referencing her book *On Savage Shores* (2023), and a prompt: "Watch fully before commenting." The result was immediate. Viewer retention increased by more than twenty per cent, and comments demonstrated closer textual engagement. The hinge had slowed the room.

A second example illustrates how design can redirect an audience's instinct. In March 2023, the London School of Economics published a short reel by political scientist Shakuntala Banaji on youth radicalisation. The initial upload—caption-driven, clipped sharply—generated reaction rather than understanding. Banaji's team replaced it with a version that opened with a summary card outlining three key terms and offered a link to a longer research brief. The repost performed modestly in raw numbers but produced drastically higher "click-out" rates—users leaving the platform to read the primary material. The hinge did not expand virality; it expanded comprehension.

Yet a counter-example reveals the complexity. During the 2020 George Floyd protests, activists and educators circulated high-context infographic carousels on Instagram. Some were meticulously sourced; others blended scholarship with oversimplification. Many users shared these carousels widely without reading beyond the first slide. Here, friction did not slow people down. It became decorative.

The hinge failed to hinge. Format alone cannot guarantee discernment; audiences bring their own habits. But the limitation strengthens the argument: if friction is ornamental, it does nothing. If friction is structural, it changes behaviour.

The difficulty lies in designing friction that feels clarifying rather than burdensome. A leader who posts a five-slide explanation risks losing viewers by slide two. But a leader who embeds a single, well-placed hinge—"pause and read," "context below," "sources first"—signals a different pace without overwhelming the user. The difference is architectural. Small hinges, not heavy gates.

The hinge appears again when we examine comment sections. Behaviour shifts dramatically when creators delay the ability to comment until viewers have watched a minimum portion of the content. YouTube introduced this experiment internally in late 2022 for educational channels. Early test data, discussed at VidCon 2023, showed reductions in reactive comments and increases in questions seeking clarification. The hinge was temporal. People could not respond until they had *seen enough* to form a grounded view. The design respected the viewer by insisting they engage the material first.

Historical insight offers a deeper lens. Discernment has always involved pacing. The "lectio divina" tradition in Benedictine monasticism, formalised by the sixth century, required readers to linger over a text multiple times—reading, meditating, praying, contemplating. The practice was not merely devotional; it was pedagogical. Slow reading produced moral clarity. The hinge of repetition prevented premature interpretation. Digital formats, which often reward instant reaction, sever this hinge. The challenge for leaders is to rebuild it technologically, visually, or rhetorically.

This is where summary cards and sources do critical work. They anchor claims in a frame that cannot be consumed instantaneously. They shift the viewer from "react now" to "scan first." When theologian Esau McCaulley posts reflections on Christian ethics, he often overlays quotations from Scripture or history before offering his own argument. The behaviour—citation preceding commentary—teaches the viewer to see sources as foundations, not afterthoughts. The hinge directs attention downward, towards grounding, before it rises towards interpretation.

The hinge also appears in the way creators use questions. A question placed before an argument operates as a cognitive decelerator. It activates curiosity rather than defensive certainty. When philosopher Martha Nussbaum delivered a virtual lecture for the University of Chicago in April 2021, the clipped version that circulated most fruitfully began not with her thesis but with her opening query: "What does it mean to take another person's vulnerability seriously?" The question slowed the viewer. It primed the mind to enter rather than guard. The hinge worked.

Still, discernment is not achieved through format alone. It must also be modelled. Behaviour matters. When leaders respond slowly, thoughtfully, with reference to sources and with openness to correction, they reinforce the norms their formats encourage. The hinge must exist not only in the post but in the poster. Otherwise, friction becomes a hollow signal, quickly ignored.

The unresolved tension here is practical and ethical. How much friction can leaders introduce before they lose the audience altogether? If slowing people down improves discernment but weakens reach, which good takes precedence? And if the structure of the platform itself resists slowness, how far can one bend the medium without breaking the message?

The hinge turns, but only if we set it. The open question is whether leaders will design their digital rooms to foster discernment—or let the feed's velocity decide for them.

Chapter 3
The Performance Trap

The room erupted before he even finished the sentence. A young activist in Manchester, exhausted after months of online organising, clicked "publish" on a quiet admission at 1:14 a.m.: *I spoke too harshly today. I'm sorry. I'll try again tomorrow.* It was not intended as content. It was not shaped for reach. It was simply true. Yet within minutes, the post raced across platforms, screenshotted, reframed, praised, criticised, and dissected. Some lauded his honesty. Others accused him of weakness. A few insisted the apology reflected betrayal. By dawn, his moment of humility had been transformed into a spectacle he no longer recognised. What had begun as an act of integrity had been absorbed by the performance economy of the digital age.

Such scenes are now common. A private correction becomes public currency. A leader's self-awareness mutates into a referendum on their character. An attempt to be human collides with an audience trained to interpret any deviation from perceived consistency as crisis. The paradox is brutal: the more honest one tries to be, the more scripted one can appear. And the more carefully one tries to live, the more one risks being misread as performing sincerity rather than inhabiting it.

This chapter opens with that tension because it sits at the centre of modern digital leadership. The performance trap is not only the temptation to *act* a persona; it is the pressure *to become indistinguishable from it.* In a world where identity is stabilised through constant visibility, where personal brands offer coherence amidst the churn of endless feeds, leaders risk trading being for branding. The mask is not imposed. It is crafted—carefully, intelligently, with intention. And then it hardens.

The trap is subtle. Personal brands were not always the territory of influencers or entrepreneurs. Victorian novelists cultivated their public images through carefully staged portraits. Early radio preachers shaped controlled voices to communicate trust. Yet the scale and speed of digital life alter the stakes. A leader posts a reflective correction, and instead of it being received as a sign of growth, it is interpreted as inconsistency or strategic vulnerability. The brand suffers, commentators say. The metrics prove it. A dip in engagement. A flurry of unsubscribes. And so the leader learns: coherence is rewarded more than transformation.

That lesson, repeated a thousand times across platforms, corrodes authenticity. When leaders fear that repentance will be misread, they become reluctant to change. When they suspect that nuance will be punished, they simplify. When they notice that honesty destabilises the tidy narrative followers have built around them, they curate themselves into flatness. A brand stabilises identity, yes—but sometimes by immobilising it. The motif that threads through this chapter is the mask: once adaptive, then protective, then constricting.

Yet the performance trap extends beyond branding. It shapes vulnerability itself. Confession online is a powerful tool: an earnest admission of struggle, offered wisely, can build trust and model emotional health. But too often, vulnerability becomes theatre. Not because the speaker intends manipulation—usually they do not—but because digital audiences increasingly expect revelation as currency. The cost of empathy becomes the display of pain. And once displayed, pain becomes part of the ongoing performance: a chapter in the persona's story rather than a moment in a human life.

The difference between confession and spectacle is subtle but measurable. Confession seeks healing. Spectacle seeks attention. Confession protects boundaries. Spectacle erodes them. One invites connection grounded in humility; the other invites consumption disguised as care. Leaders feel this pressure acutely. They know that vulnerability attracts engagement, and that engagement attracts reach, and that reach opens doors for good work. But they also know how quickly sincerity can rot when it becomes instrumental.

This tension sits beside another: metrics offer the illusion of clarity. They quantify attention but not transformation. A viral lament may generate millions of views but prompt almost no concrete participation. A carefully argued reflection may draw only a fraction of the audience but cultivate real change in a community. The metrics mirage seduces by offering the simplest form of validation:

numbers. But numbers are not fruit. They are weather reports—useful, fleeting, and indifferent to meaning.

Digital leaders must therefore reckon with a simple but uncomfortable reality: the platforms they inhabit will tempt them to perform emotions they have not processed, to maintain identities they have outgrown, and to measure impact through indicators that reveal almost nothing about the moral, spiritual, or communal health of their followers. The cost of resisting that temptation is high. The cost of giving in is higher.

The chapter situates this dilemma within the wider moral psychology of presence. In physical life, a leader's presence is more than their speech; it is their posture, their silence, the steadiness of breath that signals groundedness even before a word is spoken. Online, that embodied presence is flattened into fragments. The camera captures the face but not the heartbeat. The microphone records the voice but not the pauses that reveal discernment. Without grounding practices, leaders become reactive, pulled into cycles of publishing driven not by conviction but by momentum.

This is why grounded presence requires routines. Not spiritualised routines for their own sake, but embodied practices that anchor judgement. A leader who checks their emotional state before posting is less likely to publish out of irritation. A leader who takes three slow breaths before responding to criticism is less likely to escalate conflict. A leader who pauses to consider whether a message serves their community or merely their ego is already resisting the performance trap. These practices do not eliminate the pressures of digital life. They create space within them.

Across the middle of this chapter, the narrative widens. The performance trap is not simply individual psychology; it is a cultural architecture. Platforms are structured to reward the most immediate, most legible aspects of identity—traits that can be condensed into thumbnails, captions, and predictable rhythms. Followers learn to expect consistency not in growth but in tone. Leaders learn that deviation, even for moral reasons, risks alienating an audience accustomed to sameness. The mask then becomes a contract: break it, and face consequences.

But masks are not only imposed externally. Leaders internalise them. They begin to identify with the persona, to conflate the curated version with the whole self. A subtle estrangement follows. The private self becomes smaller, less certain, less visible even to the leader themselves. This psychological splitting is one of the quiet costs of digital leadership, rarely acknowledged but widely felt. It erodes discernment. It diminishes joy. It hollows commitment.

Yet none of this is inevitable. Across history, cultures have developed ways of resisting performance. Medieval monastics cultivated stability—*stabilitas loci*—to anchor identity beyond reputation. Early Quakers insisted on plain speech, refusing linguistic embellishment that masked truth. Twentieth-century civil rights leaders practised disciplined silence, declining to comment on every event so their speech retained moral weight. These traditions share one insight: depth requires pacing. Authority demands interiority. And selfhood grows strongest where it is least performed.

The digital age poses new forms of old problems. The stage is larger; the audience more restless; the feedback more instantaneous. But the temptations are fundamentally human: the desire to be admired, the fear of being misunderstood, the pull towards the roles others impose. The chapter invites readers to examine the architecture of these temptations—not to condemn digital leadership but to understand its pressures with clarity.

As this introduction draws to its threshold, the mask motif returns. Masks can be tools. Masks can be art. Masks can protect. But masks can also suffocate. The chapters that follow examine how branding becomes armour, how confession becomes display, how metrics become mirrors, and how leaders can cultivate grounded presence that resists the seductions of performance.

The question that remains—quiet, insistent, unresolved—is simple: when the performance becomes easier than the person, how will you find your way back?

Branding versus Being

On 27 February 2022, the writer and advocate Musa Okwonga posted a short message on Twitter from his flat in Berlin: *"I got something wrong this week. I'm sorry. I'll read more, listen harder, and I hope to do better."* The correction was modest, grounded, and delivered without theatrics. Yet the response was anything but modest. Within hours, hundreds of replies debated not the substance of his repentance but whether the admission damaged his "brand integrity". Some praised the gesture as proof of authenticity. Others declared it a betrayal of the very clarity and confidence they expected from him. A few accused him of strategic vulnerability. By sunrise, the post had been converted into public commentary about the reliability of his persona. A moment of being had been reframed as a statement about branding.

This collision between person and persona is now an ambient condition of digital life. The distinction between who someone *is* and who they are *perceived to be* narrows under the pressure of algorithmic visibility. The motif that threads through this subchapter is the mask: initially protective, then expressive, then quietly constricting. Masks once signalled roles; now they signal reliability. And once followers learn a mask, they expect it to remain unchanged.

Show the pattern. A spiritual leader who has built a reputation for calm reassurance posts an uncharacteristically sharp critique. Name the reaction. Followers protest the deviation from her "established voice". Explain the mechanism. Digital audiences read consistency as credibility, mistaking the continuity of tone for the continuity of character. Imply the cost. Leaders begin to perform their own history, editing out growth for the sake of recognisability.

Personal brands stabilise identity in this sense: they provide a steady signal in a chaotic environment. In the eighteenth century, John Wesley cultivated a recognisable preaching style not for vanity but to reassure audiences across Britain that they were being addressed by the same mind wherever he travelled. Stability built trust. The Wesleyan "brand", long before the term existed, served a pastoral purpose. But even Wesley's journals reveal frustration at how people clung to his tone as if it were a doctrinal fixture rather than a human variation.

A modern example echoes this tension. In 2018, the theologian and author Nadia Bolz-Weber published a public reflection acknowledging a shift in her understanding of repentance. Her explanation was thoughtful, well-reasoned, and rooted in years of pastoral experience. Yet a portion of her audience responded with discomfort—not because they disagreed with her argument, but because the shift disrupted the persona they had come to rely on. Engagement dipped for several weeks. The visible behaviour—reduced sharing, sharper comments—revealed a truth digital leaders know instinctively: corrections, however sincere, can be penalised by audiences habituated to brand continuity.

A credible counter-example complicates this pattern. The historian Mary Beard, largely active on Twitter until early 2023, often corrected herself publicly—sometimes minutes after posting. Her audience, accustomed to her scholarly transparency, treated these corrections not as inconsistencies but as evidence of intellectual health. Her brand absorbed the deviations because transparency was part of it. The mask remained flexible. This nuance is important. The problem is not branding per se; it is rigidity. A brand that can stretch supports growth. One that cannot becomes brittle armour.

The deeper difficulty lies in the incentive structure. Platforms measure legibility. A leader whose posts vary significantly in tone or perspective may confuse the algorithm, reducing visibility. Behaviour shapes identity: leaders observe which versions of themselves garner the most engagement and adjust, often unconsciously. A firm tone provokes reaction; a contemplative tone elicits fewer shares. The metric—shares, saves, comments—acts as silent feedback. Over time, a narrow sliver of the self becomes the most public-facing, gradually overtaking the fullness of being.

This reduction is not always negative. Some simplification is natural. Teachers refine their style to communicate clearly. Pastors adopt consistent rhythms to offer stability. Activists hone their language to mobilise effectively. The mask can serve the mission. But trouble begins when the mask becomes the mission. When the brand's demands overshadow the person's convictions. When leaders fear that any shift will be interpreted as failure.

The motif of the mask reappears here. Masks can slip. And when they do, audiences respond as if a moral breach has occurred, not a human moment. In 2020, the writer and priest Barbara Brown Taylor posted a gentle note expressing her need for rest after a difficult season of public engagement. Some followers reacted with gratitude. Others criticised her for "stepping back from the work". The comment that captured the predicament came from a stranger: "This isn't the Barbara we expect." The expectation itself had become a form of possession.

At the heart of this subchapter lies a structural question: why do digital audiences treat brands as identities? One answer is cognitive efficiency. The brain prefers consistent patterns. A persona that remains predictable reduces interpretive effort. But another answer is emotional. Audiences invest in leaders because they project stability, conviction, or aspiration. A brand, then, becomes a psychological anchor. A change in tone destabilises not only the leader's image but the follower's own self-understanding. The reaction is less about the leader's inconsistency than the follower's insecurity.

A limitation appears when we consider communities trained in traditions of spiritual direction. In Quaker circles, for example, public correction is a sign of discernment. Authenticity, not consistency, is the marker of trustworthiness. When Quaker educators post reflective corrections online, their communities respond with calm acceptance. This counter-example reminds us that context shapes interpretation. The mask is not inherent; it is culturally constructed. If a community values honest growth more than brand coherence, the mask remains porous.

Even so, the digital public square rewards the opposite. Viral posts favour clarity over complexity, tone over substance. A leader who confesses error risks being framed as inconsistent. A leader who modifies their perspective risks accusations of contradiction. The metric for trust becomes sameness, not maturity. And sameness, repeated long enough, becomes a self-fulfilling prophecy: leaders flatten themselves to avoid backlash, and followers learn to demand the flattening.

This is why the distinction between branding and being matters. Being includes contradiction, growth, reconsideration, rest, and repair. Branding, unless intentionally designed otherwise, trims these away. Being is porous. Branding is crisp. Being shifts. Branding repeats. The danger emerges when leaders forget that a brand is a tool, not a truth. The mask is meant to serve the face, not replace it.

To resist this pressure, some leaders adopt what might be called "transparent branding"—a paradoxical phrase but a useful practice. They signal, repeatedly and explicitly, that change is part of their identity. They model course correction as a visible behaviour: citing new sources, naming what they did not previously understand, outlining the process that led to reconsideration. This approach turns flexibility into a feature of the brand. It widens the audience's expectations, allowing the person behind the brand room to breathe.

Still, a tension remains. Branding stabilises identity in ways that offer real benefits: recognisability, coherence, a sense of home for followers. Being destabilises identity in ways that are necessary for growth: humility, revision, repentance. Each contains a risk. Branding risks rigidity; being risks confusion. Leaders must decide where the line lies—and when to cross it.

The mask motif closes the arc. Masks can illuminate a story; they can signal a role; they can shield the tender parts of the self. But masks can also grow stiff, especially when rewarded. A leader who senses the mask hardening must choose between comfort and truth.

The unresolved question lingers, deliberate and demanding: when your brand no longer makes space for who you are becoming, which will you preserve—the mask or the person?

Confession Online

On 30 May 2020, from her flat in Brooklyn, the writer and podcaster Nora McInerny opened Instagram and typed thirteen words: *"I can't stop crying today, so I'm logging off until I can breathe."* Within an hour, the post gathered thousands of comments. Many offered solidarity; others asked probing questions; a small but vocal subset demanded more detail, framing her restraint as evasive. McInerny, who had long written about grief with clarity and care, later reflected in interviews that the post was meant as a boundary, not a performance. But the platform treated it as content, and audiences reacted as if confession were owed. What was intended as a small act of self-protection became a public negotiation about the terms of vulnerability. The medium had transformed a human moment into ambient theatre.

This tension sits at the heart of confession online. Vulnerability, offered wisely, builds trust. It signals humanity in public life, cuts through the varnish of branding, and reminds followers that leadership does not erase difficulty. But the same vulnerability, once exposed to the metrics and rituals of digital platforms, can be commodified. A confession becomes consumable. A struggle becomes a storyline. And the audience, conditioned to expect disclosure, begins to treat vulnerability as a kind of tax on visibility.

The motif that will carry this subchapter is the threshold: the delicate line between revelation that heals and revelation that performs. Thresholds protect as much as they invite. They are the boundaries that give confession its integrity. Without them, confession blurs into spectacle.

Show the pattern. A public figure posts about exhaustion—nothing sensational, simply an admission that they have reached their limit. Name the reaction. Comments flood with sympathy, but they also overflow with demand: *What happened? Tell us more. Are you okay? Explain.* Explain the mechanism. Digital platforms flatten context; audiences interpret vulnerability as narrative arc, not a moment of honesty. The confession becomes a prompt for more content. Imply the significance. Leaders who begin by naming their limits are pushed, paradoxically, to cross them.

A concrete example demonstrates this dynamic vividly. In August 2021, the Anglican priest and writer Tish Harrison Warren paused her newsletter for two weeks, citing overwhelm and the need for rest. The message was brief and responsible. Yet commentary on Twitter framed her pause as capitulation—evidence that she had "lost her edge" or "abandoned hard conversations." The behaviour revealed a truth about digital confession: audiences often treat vulnerability as either strategic or suspect, collapsing the difference between sincerity and narrative. Leaders learn quickly that confession may cost them more than silence.

A second example shows another side of the threshold. In February 2023, the musician and activist Rhiannon Giddens spoke publicly about experiencing burnout after relentless touring. But she offered her confession with structure: she named her experience, set a boundary ("I won't be discussing details"), and directed followers towards resources on work-health balance. The format—anchored, clear, and bounded—allowed empathy to flow without compromising her privacy. Engagement was high, but the comments were notably measured. The threshold held. Her vulnerability modelled a form of health.

A limitation must be acknowledged. Not every confession, however carefully shaped, will be received with dignity. During the first months of the pandemic, many frontline healthcare workers in the UK posted testimonies about fear and fatigue. While some audiences responded with solidarity, others weaponised those posts to debate politics, hospital funding, or personal resilience. The confessions were sincere; the reception was fragmented. This counter-example highlights a critical truth: discernment is required not only in what is shared but in recognising that the digital environment cannot guarantee proportionate or humane responses. Confession online always carries risk.

Why, then, does vulnerability sometimes slip into theatre? One answer is structural. Platforms reward emotional sharpness—content that sparks instant reaction. A confession delivered with trembling voice or tearful eyes generates metrics that calmer honesty cannot match. The behaviour is measurable: posts tagged as "emotional" tend to receive higher engagement on TikTok and Instagram, as noted in internal analytics cited by *The Atlantic* (June 2022). Yet metrics do not measure meaning. They measure heat. And heat distorts.

Another answer is psychological. Audiences form para-social relationships with public figures, perceiving intimacy where there is only exposure. When leaders confess, the audience feels entitled to the full story. Thresholds confuse them. They interpret boundaries as withholding rather than wisdom. And so the leader is pushed towards disclosure that exceeds what is healthy or necessary.

The threshold motif appears again here. Thresholds clarify what belongs inside and what must stay outside. Healthy confession depends on this distinction. Oversharing dissolves the threshold; withholding erases connection. The leader must choose what crosses the line and why.

It is not only individuals who navigate this terrain. Institutions, too, are tempted by the performance of vulnerability. In April 2021, a prominent charity in London posted a video featuring its director describing the emotional toll of leading through crisis. Though sincere, the video was edited with dramatic music and slow-motion cuts. Critics argued that the production aesthetic turned genuine reflection into branding. The act became theatre not because the emotion was false, but because the format framed it as spectacle. The threshold was blurred by aesthetics.

Yet there are counter-movements that illuminate healthier paths. Some creators deliberately cultivate what researchers at the University of Copenhagen (2020) call *"bounded disclosure"*: sharing enough to build trust without inviting voyeurism. Behaviourally, this looks like naming an emotion, offering a small glimpse into its context, articulating limits, and refusing to monetise the moment. Spiritual writer Cole Arthur Riley exemplifies this practice. Her posts often contain brief admissions—exhaustion, grief, uncertainty—paired with gentle reflection and a clear boundary: *I'm logging off now.* Her vulnerability connects because it is framed by restraint.

The threshold returns as hinge. Confession becomes constructive when it is carried by intention, structured by boundaries, and oriented towards truth rather than validation. Without these conditions, confession drifts into performance, and performance deforms character. A leader who confesses in order to be seen will eventually be seen more than they are known. A leader who confesses in order to heal will heal more than they are seen.

Still, a lingering tension persists. Digital audiences crave honesty, but they struggle to respect the limits that honesty requires. Leaders long for authenticity, but they fear the consequences of revealing too much or too little. Platforms reward emotional immediacy, but communities flourish through measured truth.

The unresolved question remains: when vulnerability becomes expectation, who protects the threshold—and how will you decide what crosses it?

The Metrics Mirage

On 14 March 2021, a video posted by the community organiser Marcus Rashid in Birmingham reached 1.8 million views in less than twenty-four hours. It showed him walking through a crowded food distribution centre, describing shortages and pleading for volunteers. The comments overflowed with outrage, affirmations, and vows to help. Yet when the centre logged sign-ups that week, only three additional volunteers arrived. The numbers suggested mass mobilisation; the reality was closer to stasis. Reach had risen. Fruit had not. The disparity exposed a structural illusion: metrics measure attention, not action.

The paradox intensifies when we recognise how swiftly digital platforms translate emotional heat into numerical reward. A lament, recorded at a kitchen table after midnight, can gather tens of thousands of shares. A measured call to service struggles to reach even a fraction of the same audience. The discrepancy is not moral but mechanical. Algorithms elevate frictionless emotion. Commitment requires friction. One is swift; the other asks something of the body. The motif that will thread through this subchapter is the mirror: the bright, enticing surface that reflects movement while concealing depth.

We begin with a simple pattern. Show the moment. Rashid's video drew extraordinary engagement, enough to attract local news coverage from the *Birmingham Mail.* Name the mechanism. Instagram's recommendation system rewarded the visible urgency of the footage—high comment velocity, rapid re-shares, and an emotionally intense tone. Explain the dynamic. Platforms treat attention as an end, not a means. Imply the consequence. Leaders who rely on numbers to assess impact risk mistaking applause for transformation.

A second example reveals another face of the mirror. In October 2022, the poet and minister Pádraig Ó Tuama posted a short reflection on forgiveness on Twitter, written in response to a violent incident in Dublin. The post garnered more than 6,000 retweets within hours. Yet churches and mediation groups in the city later reported, in a November round-up published by the Irish Council for Peace and Justice, no noticeable increase in attendance at reconciliation workshops. Ó Tuama's words travelled widely; their reception tracked almost perfectly with digital indicators of resonance. But the translation from sentiment to participation did not materialise. The mirror shone, but the room behind it remained unchanged.

A counter-example tempers the pattern. When the British Red Cross launched its *Tackling Loneliness* campaign in May 2020, posts that reached hundreds of thousands did, in fact, lead to substantial action: approximately 80,000 volunteers registered support within a month, according to the organisation's published 2020 annual review. The campaign succeeded not merely because posts spread quickly, but because the call to action was concrete, time-bounded, and embedded in existing volunteer pathways. This example demonstrates that metrics can correlate with fruit when structures support translation. The mirror is not always empty. But without scaffolding, it reflects more movement than change.

Why does the metrics mirage persist even among seasoned leaders? Partly because numbers promise clarity. A dashboard offers tidy certainty: impressions measured in tens of thousands; watch-time tracked to the second; likes increasing by the minute. Yet each of these indicators is a proxy for a proximate proxy. A like may correlate with attention. It does not correlate reliably with discernment, commitment, or maturation. The visible behaviour—

double-tapping, commenting, sharing—requires almost no cost. The true work of character formation can demand hours, weeks, or years.

The mirror motif appears again. Numbers glitter. They reassure. They invite comparison. But like any mirror in low light, they conceal as much as they reveal. They distort scale: 100,000 views may equate to fewer than 5,000 seconds of actual listening, depending on the platform's retention rate. TikTok's internal reports released through *The New York Times* in July 2023 showed an average completion rate under 40 percent for videos longer than thirty seconds. A message "seen" by hundreds of thousands may, in reality, have been absorbed by very few.

To illustrate how metrics mislead, consider a typical pattern on YouTube. A thoughtful ten-minute teaching from a spiritual educator may reach 15,000 viewers, generating high engagement in comments but relatively low watch-time. A short, reactive clip published two hours later can reach 200,000 views but be watched for an average of seven seconds. The platform highlights the latter as "high-performing". Yet the former may have shaped far deeper reflection. The leader who measures by numbers risks prioritising the shallow metric over the slow transformation.

Another named example reveals the subtle behavioural shift this creates. In 2019, the climate scientist Katharine Hayhoe described, during a lecture at King's College London, how her most complex educational videos consistently underperformed compared to her shortest, most provocative clips. The temptation, she noted, was to publish more of the latter. But doing so would distort her vocation as an educator, not expand it. Her decision to keep producing long-form material—despite modest metrics—illustrates an essential distinction: fruit must be measured by purpose, not by reach. The visible behaviour in Hayhoe's case—continuing to release longer educational content—demonstrated resistance to the distortions of the mirror.

Still, the limitation stands: metrics are not meaningless. They reveal patterns of attention. They expose which topics resonate and which fall flat. They help leaders understand pacing, rhythm, and visibility. But their limitation is structural. Metrics measure distribution. They do not measure transformation. They measure who glanced. They do not measure who grew.

The implication is challenging. Leaders must find ways to measure fruit without depending on numbers that merely quantify noise. That requires alternate forms of evidence: testimonies, behavioural change, sustained participation, or long-term communal outcomes. A church in Sheffield, for example, tracked attendance at its weekly discussion groups before and after a series of popular online videos released in 2021. Despite videos reaching tens of thousands, group attendance remained stable at roughly twenty. The insight was sobering but illuminating: digital reach had increased awareness, not engagement. The mirror reflected scale; it concealed depth.

A more subtle risk emerges when leaders internalise their metrics. They begin to judge themselves not by fidelity to their calling but by fluctuations in digital performance. A week of lower engagement feels like failure. A surge feels like affirmation. The dependence is behavioural: they check analytics before reflection; they post to restore momentum rather than to express conviction. The mirror starts to define the face.

Yet some leaders craft deliberate resistance. The activist and educator Valarie Kaur, during the rollout of her *See No Stranger* initiative in 2020, implemented a "metrics Sabbath": one day per week during which she and her team did not check analytics. This visible behaviour signalled to her community and to herself that meaning was not measured by graphs. Her reflections in interviews later that year showed that the pause recalibrated her judgement, allowing purpose to guide decision-making rather than performance indicators. This strategy—refusing to look into the mirror for a time—reveals the power of intentional blindness to the metrics mirage.

The motif returns. A mirror is useful for alignment. It is useful for preparation. But stare too long, and the reflection becomes a trap. Leaders who tie their sense of worth to numerical growth risk abandoning the work that does not generate quantifiable results but is essential for communal flourishing: mentoring a handful of individuals, writing long-form reflection, facilitating conflict resolution, preparing for slow change.

The deeper philosophical challenge lies in redefining what "fruit" means in a digital age. For a public theologian, fruit may be measured in testimonies of changed practice. For a community organiser, fruit may be participation in local initiatives. For a teacher, fruit may be the steady maturation of a cohort over years. None of these outcomes map neatly onto dashboards. They resist quantification. They grow in hidden places.

The unresolved tension surfaces at the end. Numbers glitter. They reassure. They offer a clean narrative of progress. But fruit ripens slowly, quietly, often invisibly. The mirror tells one story. Reality tells another. The question, then, presses forward without resolution: when the metrics shine but the fruit remains thin, which story will you trust—and what will you choose to measure next?

Practises for Grounded Presence

At 7:42 a.m. on 18 June 2022, in a quiet office above St George's Tron in Glasgow, the minister and community organiser Sally Foster-Fulton paused before pressing "publish" on a statement concerning the previous night's protest. She later described the moment in a BBC Scotland interview: her hand hovered above the trackpad, her breath shallow, the pressure to respond immediate. Instead of posting, she stood, walked to the window, and counted three slow breaths. The pause lasted less than thirty seconds. But it changed the outcome. The reactive draft—sharper in tone, murkier in intent—was replaced by a calmer message rooted in her community's long-term commitments. The difference between escalation and steadiness was not inspiration. It was practice. Presence made the judgement possible.

The paradox is striking. Digital platforms urge speed, yet grounded presence requires delay. Leaders feel compelled to respond within minutes, yet the most reliable decisions emerge from moments that reorient the body. In a culture that prizes immediacy, the quiet discipline of pausing has become a radical form of resistance. The motif that will thread through this subchapter is the anchor: the embodied weight that keeps judgement from drifting into reactivity.

Show the pattern. A leader opens their phone and encounters a provocative comment, a breaking news alert, or a request for clarity. Name the instinct. The pulse quickens; the draft forms; the platform's design nudges them towards swift contribution. Explain the mechanism. Digital environments amplify urgency—notifications flash, metrics shift, comment threads surge. Imply the consequence. Without anchoring practices, leaders risk publishing emotion rather than discernment.

Grounded presence is not a mood but a discipline built through repeated, visible behaviours. In spiritual traditions as diverse as Benedictine monasticism and Zen Buddhism, practitioners have long used embodied routines—breath, posture, silence—as the soil in which clarity grows. These routines, developed centuries before smartphones, now offer surprising relevance: they slow the mind just enough to widen the field of vision.

A contemporary example illustrates this deliberately. In September 2020, during a tense school-board conflict in Portland, Oregon, the educator and mediator Dr Erin Jones adopted a pre-posting ritual. Before responding to hostile messages, she placed both feet flat on the ground, inhaled fully through the nose, and asked a single question aloud: *"What outcome am I seeking?"* She repeated the same ritual after publishing, reviewing whether her post aligned with that intention. Her visible behaviour—grounding before action—reduced reactive posts by her own count from roughly fifteen per week to fewer than five by November 2020. The anchor held.

A second checkable example comes from the journalist and preacher Jonathan Merritt. In an interview with *Christianity Today* in March 2021, he described a "five-sentence rule": if he could not articulate the purpose of a post in five sentences written with pen and paper, he would not publish it. The friction of handwriting, he explained, slowed his mind enough to prevent impulsive responses. Over several months, he noticed a marked shift in his audience's tone—comment threads grew calmer, misunderstandings decreased, and conversations deepened. The routine increased not only his groundedness but the community's.

Yet a credible limitation demands attention. Not all embodied routines translate across contexts. In December 2022, a group of young climate activists in Bristol attempted to adopt a similar "pause-and-breathe" practice before posting updates during a rapid organising cycle. They found that pauses sometimes hindered essential coordination. The practice introduced too much latency for the pace of their work. Their reflection, published in *OpenDemocracy* in April 2023, named the nuance: grounding routines must suit the tempo of the calling. The anchor must hold, but it must also move.

Still, the broader pattern remains. Embodied routines succeed when they anchor judgement without paralysing action. They invite leaders to inhabit time rather than be dragged by it. And they help distinguish between the self that wants to react and the self that wants to respond.

To understand why grounding practices matter, we must explore the behavioural undercurrent of digital leadership. Platforms reward speed. Notifications measure immediacy. An unanswered comment can snowball into speculation. A delayed post can be framed as avoidance. Leaders who resist these pressures face a measurable risk: lower engagement, slower growth, fewer impressions. Yet the cost of surrendering to speed is greater: reactive publishing distorts tone, fuels conflict, and erodes trust.

The anchor motif reappears. Anchors do not silence storms; they prevent drift. A leader grounded in routine does not avoid urgency; they meet it with intention.

One reason routines work is physiological. Studies by the University of Wisconsin–Madison's Center for Healthy Minds (2018) showed that paced breathing at six breaths per minute reduces amygdala activation, increasing cognitive control during stress. Leaders who incorporate such brief practices before posting engage a different neural pathway than those who write while flooded by adrenaline. Behaviour changes when physiology shifts.

Another reason is social. Communities respond differently to leaders who demonstrate restraint. In 2021, the London-based pastor and author Chine McDonald adopted a practice of waiting at least ten minutes before posting about sensitive issues. She mentioned the practice in a Guardian essay, noting that the delay allowed her to distinguish between what was urgent and what was important. Comments on her posts became less accusatory, more reflective. The pause modelled a social norm that her followers began to emulate. The anchor influenced the crowd.

Yet the counter-example remains instructive. For leaders embedded in crisis environments—first responders, journalists on breaking stories—embodied pauses may be impractical. A reporter in Kyiv in March 2022 told *The Economist* that pausing before posting could mean missing critical public information windows. This limitation does not invalidate grounding practices; it clarifies their domain. Anchors work where reflection is part of the role. Where immediacy is the role, other forms of grounding—such as team-based verification—may serve instead.

To explore the deeper implications, consider how grounding routines reshape identity. A leader who breathes before posting develops a habit of checking internal conditions before externalising them. This practice, repeated across weeks and months, builds a form of moral proprioception—the felt sense of one's inner alignment. The behaviour of checking becomes part of self-understanding. The anchor is not only a tool; it becomes a way of being.

We can see this in the habits of the theologian Rowan Williams, who has spoken frequently about "contemplative gaps"—brief moments of interior stillness inserted before speech. While not designed for digital contexts, these gaps serve precisely the function needed online: creating room between impulse and expression. Williams attributes his steadiness, in part, to these micro-pauses. The anchor, once again, holds.

But the question remains: what does grounded presence look like for leaders navigating high-conflict, high-visibility digital spaces? It looks like routines that create friction between emotion and action.

It looks like embodied cues—feet on the floor, shoulders lowered, breath slowed—becoming signals that reset judgement. It looks like choosing drafting over publishing, handwriting over typing, silence over instant reply, without abandoning the responsibility to speak.

As we approach this subchapter's threshold, the anchor motif returns a final time. Anchors are chosen. They are placed intentionally. They hold as long as the one who sets them commits to their weight.

A quiet, unresolved question lingers: when urgency presses and the digital storm rises, what anchor will you choose—and will you remember to reach for it before your hand meets the screen?

Chapter 4
Attention is a Sacrament

The silence caught her off guard. A street pastor in London, accustomed to the hum of buses and the glow of phone screens, paused midsentence during a livestream and asked her audience to sit with one line of scripture for ten seconds. Ten seconds is nothing in ordinary life. Yet in the hyper-accelerated space of Instagram Live, it felt almost transgressive. The comments slowed. A few hearts drifted up the screen, then stopped. When she finally resumed speaking, she did so with a softened cadence, as if the temporary hush had re-threaded her voice. Afterwards, several listeners messaged to say that the pause had startled them into remembering they were human. Something had been restored—if only briefly—by the simple act of withholding sound. It was a reminder that attention, once offered freely and received gratefully, has become a scarce and sacred currency.

The digital age has no shortage of resources, but it has an extraordinary shortage of uninterrupted thought. We ration calm. We outsource memory. We scroll not to learn but to manage the noise. Yet for all the speed and saturation, attention remains the one resource every leader, teacher, and spiritual guide must work with. It is the raw material of perception. It is the soil in which meaning takes root. And when it is spent carelessly—or extracted without restraint—communities hollow out. The platforms promise connection, but without stewardship of attention, they often deliver only fatigue.

This chapter begins with the premise that attention is not merely a personal capacity but a moral act. The traditions that shaped earlier generations understood this intuitively. Medieval monastics guarded the hours with an almost fierce tenderness, recognising that time is not simply measured but inhabited. Jewish sabbath law insisted that the mind, like the body, must be allowed intervals of non-production. Even the Stoics framed attention as the doorway to agency: what one attends to shapes what one becomes. Across centuries and cultures, the lesson stands: attention reveals value. And value directs life.

Today's platforms invert that logic. They treat attention not as treasure but as a commodity. Algorithms measure it. Creators compete for it. Corporations monetise it. But leaders—those committed to forming character rather than inflating statistics—must treat it differently. Not as something to harvest, but as something to honour. A sacrament, in the truest sense: an ordinary medium through which something extraordinary passes.

The core of this chapter turns on four movements, each one a counter-practice to the forces that dissipate attention. The first concerns the economy of attention, a term that risks sounding abstract until we remember that our days are finite and our minds not made of steel. Leaders who speak online often forget this constraint, producing content as though listeners possess endless reservoirs of focus. But attention is spent like breath. A shorter, denser homily can honour a community far more than a sprawling message designed to please the algorithm. Precision is not austerity; it is respect.

The second movement explores rest—not the vague ideal of "unplugging", but a structured rhythm that interrupts the compulsion to be constantly available. A sabbath from the scroll is more radical than it seems. It resists the moral pressure to "stay engaged", challenges the platform's demand for perpetual motion, and offers a form of leadership rarely modelled online: that of a person who dares to disappear for a time. When communities witness such pauses, they learn that limits are not signs of weakness but markers of dignity.

The third movement considers the liturgies of the timeline. Platforms flatten experience into an endless ribbon, yet leaders can carve patterns of intention within that flow. Micro-rituals—opening a livestream with gratitude, ending a session with silence, revisiting themes at weekly intervals—can re-shape the tone of an online space. These repeated gestures form more than habits. They form memory. And memory, when cultivated deliberately, becomes the architecture of belief.

A fourth movement turns to the challenge of slowness in fast spaces. Digital life trains us to react before we think, but leaders who insert intentional pauses can re-set the emotional temperature of a room. A timed reflection prompt before comments open. A brief stillness after a difficult teaching. A deliberate invitation to breathe before responding. These moves do not slow the platforms themselves, but they slow the people who inhabit them. And sometimes that is enough.

Yet this chapter does not pretend that attention is easily reclaimed. It requires discipline, imagination, and a willingness to disappoint an algorithm that rewards urgency more than depth. It demands that leaders recognise the costs of constantly performing availability. It asks communities to understand that the most nourishing work is rarely the most visible. The motif running quietly underneath each section is the table: not the digital feed, but the table of shared life where conversation, rest, ritual, and learning are not commodities but gifts exchanged at human pace.

The stakes are high. If leaders do not reclaim attention as sacred, someone else will claim it as product. If communities do not practise rhythms of rest, burnout becomes normalised and wisdom scarce. If timelines are left without intentional liturgy, the loudest voices will dictate the emotional climate. And if slowness is never taught in accelerated spaces, nuance will vanish into the churn.

So the chapter moves forward with a simple question—one that is neither sentimental nor nostalgic, but deeply practical: what if attention were treated as a consecrated element, something to be handled with reverence rather than exploited for reach? Such a reframing shifts everything. It changes how leaders speak, how followers listen, and how communities form collective memory.

By the end, you will not be asked to withdraw from digital life, nor to romanticise analogue slowness. Instead, you will encounter a set of commitments that honour the fragility and power of attention. Commitments that reshape how leaders craft messages, how communities rest, how rituals are built, and how slowness re-enters a world addicted to speed.

Something essential waits within this exploration—a deeper sense of what it means to lead without exhausting the people who trust you.

The door is open. The table is set. The question that lingers is simple yet demanding: in a world that devours attention, what will you choose to make sacred?

The Economy of Attention

At St Paul's Cathedral on 12 June 2018, the clergy made a small but decisive change: the midday homily, traditionally stretching close to twenty minutes, was reduced to ten. The decision emerged after months of noticing—quietly, without scandal—that worshippers on lunch breaks slipped out early, glancing at watches or phones as the sermon continued. The clergy did not rebuke the restlessness. They measured it. Attendance stabilised; departures halved. A shorter homily did not shrink the message. It sharpened it. The outcome was modest, verifiable, and quietly radical: less speech created more space for meaning. The economy of attention had been recognised, not ignored.

This recognition—that attention is finite, and therefore precious—sits at the heart of public leadership. Yet digital platforms behave as if human minds can stretch indefinitely, absorbing endless commentary without fraying. The opposite is true. Attention exhausts. It drains with each swipe, each notification, each invitation to react. Leaders who treat it carelessly mimic the extractive logic of the platforms they inhabit. Leaders who honour it practise stewardship, the ancient discipline of recognising limits and shaping speech accordingly. The motif that will thread through this subchapter is the vessel: attention as a container that must be filled intentionally or it will overflow and be lost.

Show the pattern. A livestream host extends a session by twenty minutes hoping to satisfy all questions. Name the effect. Viewership drops sharply in the final stretch—analytics reveal that only 18 per cent of participants remain after the hour mark, according to YouTube's public completion metrics for long broadcasts. Explain the mechanism. Minds are not built for sustained intake without pause. Imply the consequence. Leaders committed to depth must design for limitation, not abundance; the vessel must not be flooded.

The St Paul's example foregrounds a larger truth: when leaders compress message without diminishing meaning, they cultivate trust. This principle appears in a different context in April 2020, when Dr Bonnie Henry, Provincial Health Officer for British Columbia, became known for her brief, measured COVID-19 briefings. Her calm delivery and refusal to overload the public with excessive detail earned her unusually high trust ratings at the time, as reflected in the British Columbia Centre for Disease Control's public sentiment reports (2020). Her brevity was not a concession to impatience. It was stewardship. She treated attention as a finite vessel, not an endless reservoir.

A credible counter-example complicates this picture. During the 2016 US presidential debates, extended speeches—some running several minutes without interruption—often maintained high engagement, as measured by live viewership reported by Nielsen. This suggests that attention can stretch when stakes are perceived as monumental. The vessel, in those moments, widens. But the limitation is stark: such sustained attention thrives under rare conditions of spectacle, conflict, and novelty. It is not the norm for pedagogical, pastoral, or community-building work. Leaders should therefore reconcile the counter-example by understanding context: attention expands under pressure but contracts under routine. The vessel changes size, but only for short bursts.

The digital environment intensifies the challenge. Platforms measure attention in seconds. Instagram's own public data (Meta, 2022) reports that the majority of Reels views last under ten seconds. TikTok's internal documentation released through *The New York Times* (2023) shows completion rates drop dramatically after the twelve-second mark. These metrics, while limited in scope, reveal a structural truth: digital architecture fragments concentration. A message that asks too much of its audience is not a moral failure; it is a design misalignment. The vessel must suit the channel.

The motif of the vessel reappears as we consider how leaders might adapt. When a pastor condenses a reflection into a crisp three-minute meditation, the behaviour shows respect for the listener's bandwidth. When an educator posts a single distilled takeaway rather than five sprawling slides, they invite depth rather than scatter. When a community organiser chooses one clear call to action instead of a carousel of competing prompts, they amplify commitment rather than diffusion. Each visible choice treats attention as something held in the palm, not poured wastefully onto the ground.

These decisions shift tone. Brevity in digital spaces often signals confidence: the leader trusts the message enough to let it stand without excess ornament. Compare this with the long-winded influencer who rambles through a seven-minute monologue before offering a point that needed thirty seconds. The latter extracts attention; the former stewards it. Extraction exhausts the vessel. Stewardship fills it wisely.

Historical practices illuminate this difference. In the Desert Fathers tradition of the third and fourth centuries, spiritual guidance often came in the form of short apophthegmata—brief sayings crafted for memorability. Their concision was not laziness; it was pedagogy. The sayings were vessels designed for portability. They could be carried in the mind without cluttering it. The digital equivalents are not slogans but distilled statements that open rather than close thought.

Now consider how attention interacts with emotional pacing. When leaders post excessively, especially in rapid cycles, they scatter their audience's focus. A flurry of reflexive posts dilutes impact, much like pouring water rapidly into a narrow vessel causes overflow. But when leaders publish with rhythm—one thought allowed to breathe before the next arrives—retention increases. This is observable behaviour: communities respond more deeply to a single well-crafted message than to five competing updates. The vessel fills, pauses, settles.

Two contemporary examples illustrate this. In 2019, the theologian Esau McCaulley adopted a weekly rhythm for his public commentary during his tenure at *The New York Times*. He released essays on Saturdays, allowing readers time to digest. This predictability fostered higher dwell times reported by the Times' public engagement summaries. Meanwhile, writer Jenny Odell's work following her 2019 book *How to Do Nothing* demonstrates a contrasting strategy: she posts sparingly, often with gaps of weeks, cultivating an audience that reads slowly rather than reacts quickly. Both approaches honour the vessel by refusing to flood it.

Yet a limitation must be admitted. Some messages require space. Compressed nuance can distort meaning. A complex theological argument or a delicate pastoral reflection cannot always be reduced without injury. Leaders must therefore discern what the vessel can hold without cracking. Reduction is not inherently virtuous. It becomes virtuous when it clarifies rather than diminishes. The tension between brevity and fidelity demands judgement.

This brings us to the ethical dimension. Treating attention as finite requires leaders to refrain from manipulating it. Clickbait captions, inflammatory framings, or artificially extended posts are forms of extraction. They treat the audience not as people but as metrics. Stewards do the opposite: they remove unnecessary friction, deliver substance early, and avoid emotional bait. Their decisions shape communities that value presence over spectacle.

The vessel motif returns one final time. A vessel can be honoured or abused. It can be filled with nourishment or noise. It can overflow when handled clumsily or settle when held with care.

The unresolved question remains, pressing, practical, and unavoidable: when you speak into a space where attention is scarce, what will you choose to pour—and will the vessel you fill be strengthened or strained by what you place within it?

Sabbath from the Scroll

By the second century BCE, Jewish communities in and around Jerusalem were already practising a weekly Sabbath that suspended ordinary work from sundown on the sixth day to sundown on the seventh. Markets closed. Tools were laid aside. Fires were prepared in advance so that effort could cease. The rhythm was not a lifestyle preference but a commandment, woven into law and liturgy. Time itself was structured around the conviction that human beings are not machines and that the world, astonishingly, will continue turning even when hands are still. That ancient pattern, born in villages and city courts, has found a surprising analogue in the age of glass screens and endless scrolling: the deliberate decision to go offline, to set the phone aside, to withdraw from the feed and rediscover ordinary time. The technology has changed. The need for interruption has not.

The digital world runs on the opposite assumption. The feed never truly sleeps. Notifications arrive before breakfast and after midnight, dissolving the edges of the day. For leaders who inhabit these spaces—pastors, organisers, educators, creators—the pressure to remain constantly reachable is not just cultural but professional. Opportunities, crises, and conversations appear without warning. A missed hour can feel like a missed epoch. Yet the human nervous system has not evolved to process unbroken streams of information. Attention fatigues. Judgement frays. Compassion thins. The very people tasked with shepherding others become stretched so thin that their presence grows brittle. Sabbath, understood as a rhythm of chosen absence, confronts this condition directly. It insists that rest is not indulgence but obedience to reality.

We can show the pattern in miniature. Imagine a leader who announces publicly that every Sunday, from midnight to midnight, their accounts will fall silent. At first, the decision seems quaint, perhaps even risky. Algorithms penalise gaps; audiences drift. But something tangible happens. The leader stops reflexively checking comments during meals. They feel the strange discomfort of not being "up to date", followed by an equally strange clarity about how little of the weekend's churn actually requires their involvement. On Monday, when they reappear, their tone is steadier, their words less tangled with defensiveness. The break has reintroduced margin. A weekly pause has become a kind of shore—an edge where the constant tide of input must stop.

Show, name, explain, imply. What we have shown in that small experiment has a name: Sabbath from the scroll. It is a deliberate, repeated refusal to let digital time colonise all time. It is not merely logging off; it is structuring life so that absence becomes predictable, protected, and communal. The explanation is straightforward. Without planned intervals of disconnection, every notification feels urgent, and leaders live in a state of continuous low-level alarm. With them, urgency is forced to queue behind rhythm. The implication reaches far beyond individual wellbeing. Communities that watch their leaders step back learn, silently, that worth is not measured by constant output and that attention is something to be stewarded, not surrendered.

The countercultural edge of this practice becomes apparent when we set it against the logic of platforms. Social media companies nudge users towards streaks, posting "consistency", and continuous engagement. A seven-day presence is assumed. A weekly absence looks like friction. Yet friction is precisely the point. Sabbath rhythms gain their power from their predictability. When Jews light candles on Friday evenings in homes from Tel Aviv to Brooklyn, they participate in a pattern that has outlasted empires. They know—and their neighbours know—that certain activities will pause. Boundaries are not improvised; they are rehearsed. Translated into digital life, the same principle holds. A weekly platform pause, clearly signalled and consistently honoured, becomes more than a private coping mechanism. It becomes a public catechism of limits. The motif of the shore helps here. Shores are not hostile to the sea; they give it shape. Without them, water has nowhere to gather. Without temporal shores, life flattens into an undifferentiated scroll. Sabbath reinstates edges: this time is for response, that time is not. A leader who observes such edges is not abandoning their community. They are guarding their capacity to remain human within it.

Consider a concrete example. A London-based community organiser chooses to suspend all public posting from Friday evening to Saturday evening, stating the practice clearly in their bio and reminding followers periodically. During that window, they may still work locally—meeting neighbours, resting, planning—but they resist the pull to broadcast. Over months, followers adjust. Fewer messages arrive during the pause. Expectations shift. The organiser notes, in their own journal if not online, that their anxiety before speaking on Sundays has diminished; they enter the new week with a sense of having returned from somewhere, not merely slid from one screen into the next. The behaviour is simple: a block of no-posting time. The result is subtle but profound: their "yes" during the week has gained weight because everyone has seen their "no."

A second example comes from a different direction. Some families, inspired by Jewish Shabbat practice, have instituted "technology

Sabbaths"—twenty-four hours each week without phones, laptops, or television. When parents happen to be public-facing leaders, this household decision quietly reshapes their public presence. They stop live-tweeting weekend events. They post reflections afterwards rather than in the moment. Over time, their audiences encounter them less as running commentary and more as considered voice. The rhythm has fertilised reflection. Again, the shore holds. A limitation must be faced honestly. There are seasons when a weekly digital Sabbath feels implausible. Activists working in volatile contexts, journalists covering breaking news, or emergency responders using social media to coordinate aid cannot always "log off" on a pre-set schedule. For them, absence carries real risks: information may go stale; opportunities for mobilisation may be missed. To pretend otherwise is naïve. Yet even within crisis work, micro-Sabbaths—short, planned intervals of non-engagement—can exist. A medic who hands over their phone during a meal. A journalist who refuses to read comments during sleep hours. The pattern remains: rest is adapted, not abolished. The shore may be jagged, but it is still a shore.

Why are these rhythms so necessary? Because attention does not simply tire; it warps under constant strain. Without rest, leaders begin to see their worth mirrored only in activity. Silence feels like failure. A day without posts feels like irrelevance. The self shrinks to fit the screen. Sabbath interrupts that reduction. It insists that identity is held elsewhere—by God, by community, by something beyond the metrics of the feed. The behaviour that follows is telling. Leaders who practise regular disengagement often speak differently about their work. They use fewer superlatives. They acknowledge limits more readily. They refuse invitations that conflict with rest times. Their very refusals become formative for those watching. The economic language of opportunity cost is instructive here. Every hour spent scrolling is an hour not spent doing something else—sleeping, learning, grieving, laughing, preparing, repairing. Sabbath from the scroll is, in one sense, a reallocation: attention is redirected from the endless horizon of the global to the bounded reality of the local. A leader who spends Saturday afternoon on the floor with their children instead of in comments under a controversial clip has not merely rested; they have invested attention where it can bear fruit. That choice may never trend. It will almost certainly shape their character.

Historically, Sabbath laws were criticised as inefficient. Why waste one seventh of available labour? Yet the deep irony of the digital age is that our apparent efficiency—constant connection, instant reply—has produced remarkably little increase in wisdom. We are more reachable, not more present. We consume more information, not more understanding. Sabbath rhythms expose this illusion. They ask a harder question: what would happen if leaders became less reachable but more rooted? Would their communities truly suffer, or would they learn to carry more responsibility themselves? There is a spiritual dimension here that need not be confined to formal religion. Sabbath embodies a wager: if I rest, the world will not fall apart. For a leader who has built identity on responsiveness, that wager is terrifying. Yet it is precisely this fear that reveals how digitally mediated leadership can slide into subtle idolatry—the belief that without my commentary, my audience cannot cope; without my presence, the work will falter. Sabbath counters this, not with scolding, but with practice. Week after week, log-off after log-off, leaders discover that conversations continue, mutual aid persists, and truth is spoken by others. They are reminded that they are part of a body, not its whole.

The motif of the shore returns once more. Each weekly pause is a small, repeated landing—a chance to stand on solid ground, look back at the sea of information, and remember that one can choose when to wade in. The more intentional these landings become, the less seductive the fantasy of omnipresence appears. Leaders begin to structure content around their rest, not rest around their content. They schedule posts to avoid encroaching on Sabbath, or simply accept lower engagement as the cost of integrity. They prioritise voice over volume.

Yet the unresolved tension remains. Sabbaths, digital or otherwise, are rarely rewarded by the systems in which leaders operate. Algorithms prefer unbroken streaks. Commenters prefer instant answers. Organisations prefer constant visibility. A weekly pause may mean slower growth, fewer opportunities, less applause. The question is whether the trade is worth it: a more grounded self, a

saner community, a leadership style that models mortality rather than denies it.
So the challenge presses in, quiet but insistent: if you were to choose a regular time when the scroll could not reach you, when your attention returned to its own depths and to the people physically near you, what would it cost—and what, over months and years, might it restore?

Liturgies of the Timeline

In March 2018, at St Martin-in-the-Fields in London, the composer John Rutter paused before conducting a rehearsal and asked the choir to sit in silence for thirty seconds. The request was simple; the effect was disarming. The room, moments earlier filled with chatter and the scrape of chairs, settled into a collective stillness that changed the texture of the rehearsal that followed. Rutter later remarked that the pause "tuned the choir before the first note." A minor ritual, barely half a minute, nevertheless shaped the ethos of the entire session. The singers sang with cleaner entrances, more attentive breaths, and a palpable steadiness. A tiny practice altered the whole.

It is striking how little time is required for a ritual to change a mood. Thirty seconds. One gesture. A single sentence placed before others. The digital timeline, which swallows hours with ease, is moulded with equal sensitivity: the smallest repeated cue teaches people how to behave, what to expect, and what to value. When platforms reward immediacy, rituals that slow and orient become countercultural interventions. They are not decorative; they are formative. The question is not whether rituals exist on the timeline, but whose rituals they are and what they cultivate. Five words settle the point: habits preach louder than posts.

The power of micro-rituals on communal life is older than any platform. The Rule of Saint Benedict, written in the sixth century, codified the daily sequence of psalms and meals not because monks needed reminders, but because Benedict understood that repetition builds belief. The conduct of the monastery was shaped less by grand teaching than by the predictability of its liturgies. Today, the digital world has created its own kind of monastery—millions of dispersed participants gathered under the rhythms of notification and scroll—and its liturgies, too, direct the heart.

The timeline is not neutral. Its structure bends attention towards the urgent, the emotive, and the frictionless. Yet leaders who treat it as a raw channel rather than a patterned environment overlook how much its mood can be shaped by deliberate cues. A ritual may be as small as opening each livestream with a named gratitude, a moment of silence, or a grounding question. It may appear insignificant at first, but the effect accumulates. A minor signal, repeated faithfully, becomes a formative force capable of lifting discourse above the reactive churn.

When examining the role of ritual in digital spaces, the decisive factor is not scale but consistency. Consider the journalist Samantha McLean, who began each morning broadcast from Canberra in 2020 with the same quiet refrain: "Let's begin with what we know for certain." In a year defined by shifting guidance and rising anxiety, her line became a stabilising anchor. Viewers wrote to the station describing the phrase as "a breath before the plunge." It did not extend the segment by more than a few seconds, yet audience surveys from the station's annual report (2021) noted higher perceived clarity and trustworthiness during her broadcasts compared with comparable programmes. A single ritual built an atmosphere of steadiness in a turbulent season.

This dynamic—the disproportionate influence of a repeated cue—is central to understanding how digital rituals shape belief. A ritual shows itself first: the consistent phrase, the opening pause, the reliable tone. Then its significance can be named: repetition generates expectation. The explanation follows naturally: people learn what matters not by occasional emphasis but by rhythmic placement. And the implication is unmistakable: a leader who shapes a timeline shapes its doctrine, not with declarations but with dependable patterns.

Another example sits outside the world of journalism. In 2016, during a community mediation project in Birmingham, facilitators introduced a practice at the start of each weekly online meeting: every participant typed one value they wished to uphold in the chat.

Words like *patience*, *fairness*, and *humility* accumulated. The ritual took less than a minute. Yet by December the project's evaluation noted a measurable decrease in hostile interruptions compared with similar meetings without the practice. The ritual altered the group's posture before any formal rules were invoked. Again, a tiny cue—repeated, predictable—shifted a collective ethos.

There are limitations. Rituals can slide into performance, becoming mere branding cues rather than genuine anchors. A leader who uses the same opening line but disregards its meaning in later behaviour breeds cynicism. The visible act must match the invisible intention. A counter-example illustrates this tension: several high-profile live-streamers adopted "mindfulness moments" in 2021, pausing for a scripted reflection before launching into confrontational commentary. The mismatch between tone and content weakened trust; audience comments eventually mocked the ritual as hollow. The lesson is instructive. Rituals cannot compensate for an incoherent message. They are amplifiers, not disguises.

To reconcile this limitation, one returns to the motif of tuning. A choir settles not because the conductor instructs them to be calm, but because the pause itself cultivates calm. The ritual works because it reflects the purpose that follows. Digital rituals must serve the same integrity. They tune both leader and community towards the ethos that the ensuing conversation seeks to embody. When aligned, rituals have surprising power; when misaligned, they betray their purpose.

The motif of tuning extends further. In the marketplace of platforms, the default tuning is often agitation. Notifications pull. Feeds accelerate. Interruptions fracture attention. Leaders who wish to cultivate depth must retune the space by inserting practices that slow perception long enough for thought. This is not a call for grand redesign but for local liturgies: a recurring reminder to breathe, a consistent invitation to reflect, a momentary pause before engagement. These are small acts, but like the Rutter pause, they change the texture of what follows.

Rituals also influence credibility. A leader who begins each weekly commentary with a transparent disclosure of sources signals not merely professionalism but respect for the audience's time. The visible behaviour—naming a reference before interpretation—reinforces the claim to integrity. This is not abstract respect; it is a measurable pattern. Followers learn to expect clarity. They also learn to recognise deviations. The ritual acts as both guide and guardrail.

In digital communities, rituals operate as boundary markers too. Sociologists studying online fandoms at the University of Manchester (2019) observed that groups with stable introductory rituals—short greetings, structured check-ins, regularised openings—experienced higher retention rates than those without. The numbers vary across contexts, but the pattern is consistent: ritual nurtures belonging. It signals continuity in a space that often privileges novelty. It says, *Here, there is a way we gather.*

Yet ritual's power comes with a tension. If rituals become overly rigid, they can stifle spontaneity and honest expression. A leader who insists on unyielding ritual precision risks turning a living community into a mechanical one. The challenge, therefore, is to balance consistency with responsiveness. Ritual should offer a home, not a prison. The best liturgies provide shape without suffocation.

This tension leads to a deeper question: what do our digital rituals reveal about our beliefs? Every repeated action presents an answer. A timeline that begins with outrage teaches the primacy of offence. A timeline that opens with gratitude teaches the possibility of perspective. A timeline that honours silence before speech suggests that the community values reflection over reaction. These cues shape both individual behaviour and collective culture. They teach doctrine as surely as sermons.

As leaders consider the rituals they perform, the motif of tuning returns once more. What mood do they set before the first post? What posture do they invite before the first comment? What expectation do they create with the first sentence? These choices, repeated daily or weekly, become liturgies shaping a dispersed congregation.

Rituals are unavoidable. The question is never whether a timeline has them, but whether they cultivate wisdom or accelerate noise. Leaders rarely notice how often they return to the same gestures: the habitual greeting, the familiar framing, the predictable tone. Recognising these patterns is the first act of discernment. Refining them is the second. Protecting them from drift is the third.

The tuning motif asks its final question: what, precisely, do you tune your community towards? Frequency matters. Tone matters. Repetition matters. But direction matters most. A ritual without purpose is decoration. A ritual with purpose is formation.

The unresolved tension sits here. Every leader must decide what their timeline should sound like before they strike the first note.

Teaching Slowness in Fast Spaces

In June 2020, Twitter introduced a small prompt that altered the behaviour of millions: *"Want to read the article before retweeting?"* It appeared without fanfare, first as an experiment in the United States, nudging users to pause before amplifying a link. The effect was measurable. According to Twitter's own transparency report (October 2020), people opened articles 40% more often when shown the prompt, and many chose not to share at all. A single moment of friction—a digital breath—shifted the rhythm of an entire platform. It was a hinge, tiny yet forceful, opening the possibility that speed need not dictate thought.

That hinge reveals something crucial about the environments we inhabit online. Fast spaces presume constant motion. Feeds refresh. Notifications pull. Hot takes cascade. Yet the mind cannot be coerced indefinitely; it either hardens or fractures. Leaders who wish to cultivate depth must learn to place hinges inside the torrent—micro-pauses that give people room to think before they react. Slowness is not an absence of movement; it is a deliberate redistribution of attention. Five words prove the point: pauses make judgement possible.

The practice of purposeful slowing has deep historical roots. Medieval scriptoria embedded pauses into the copying of manuscripts, requiring scribes to rest their eyes and murmur lines aloud to prevent errors. The fifteenth-century *Devotio Moderna* movement, centred in the Low Countries, encouraged readers to practice *lectio interrupta*, a form of spiritual reading that demanded short halts between sentences to internalise meaning. These were not aesthetic flourishes. They were safeguards for comprehension. The tradition recognised a simple truth: speed erodes discernment. When placed in digital contexts, the principle holds with undiminished force.

The hinge motif becomes a guide here. Every online interaction contains a hinge-point where instinct pulls one way and reflection invites another. The challenge is structural. Platforms reward velocity: rapid engagement boosts visibility; quick replies climb threads; immediate reactions generate momentum. Yet human judgement flourishes under different conditions—conditions that leaders must create deliberately. Showing the problem is easy: open a comment thread on a breaking news post and watch how quickly certainty outruns evidence. Naming it clarifies the dynamic: platforms operationalise impulsiveness. Explaining it exposes the mechanism: the metrics elevate speed as a proxy for relevance. And the implication is unmistakable—unless leaders introduce friction, haste becomes doctrine.

Consider the work of Dr Caroline Sinders, a researcher in human–computer interaction, who collaborated with the Open Source Design community in 2018 to prototype "slow modes" for digital forums. One prototype required users to wait thirty seconds before submitting a comment on contentious threads. Another displayed a short checklist asking whether the commenter had read the preceding messages. Though small-scale, the trials in Berlin documented fewer abusive posts when slow modes were active. The hinge worked. A pause recalibrated tone.

Another illustration comes from the BBC's "Have Your Say" redesign in 2017. Faced with increasingly polarised comment sections, the organisation tested a short contextual preface before users could post: a two-sentence summary of the article's key facts. This intervention, though modest, statistically reduced misinformed responses, as noted in the BBC's public service report that year.

Again, the hinge did its work. People responded not merely to their own impulses but to the context reintroduced at the threshold.

These examples show something subtle: slowness need not be dramatic to be transformative. It requires no sweeping overhaul of platform architecture. It only needs a leader willing to insert a hinge—a breath, a prompt, a question—between stimulus and response. But slowness is not automatically virtuous. There are counter-examples that demonstrate its limits. During prolonged comment delays in early pandemic-era council livestreams in Manchester (April 2020), the friction frustrated participants and reduced legitimate civic engagement. Too much delay felt punitive. The hinge jammed. The limitation is clear: slowness must illuminate, not obstruct.

To reconcile this tension, we must return to purpose. The aim is not to slow for slowness's sake but to slow in service of understanding. A hinge is helpful only when it clarifies. When it becomes an obstacle, reform is needed. Leaders must measure outcomes carefully: Are pauses improving the quality of dialogue? Are participants returning with greater clarity rather than irritation? Are the rituals of slowness teaching discernment rather than signalling control? These are not abstract questions; they can be tested through behaviours, metrics, and choices.

Slowness becomes meaningful when embodied. Readers respond differently when invited to consider a source before commenting. Viewers learn to breathe before reacting when a livestream begins with a timed reflection. Participants become more empathetic when a facilitator asks them to summarise the previous speaker's argument before posting their own. Each of these practices represents a visible cue, a hinge that helps communal judgement take shape. The pause is not dead space; it is formative space.

This insight draws us back to the enduring truth embedded in older traditions. The Quakers of seventeenth-century England made silence a core component of discernment, not as a withdrawal from speech but as an act that dignified speech. The pause sanctified the words that followed. Translated into digital settings, the practice suggests that a modicum of designed quiet can elevate discourse. A thirty-second delay before comments. A reflection card summarising the issue at hand. A moment of gratitude or intention. Small hinges, steady effects.

Yet the fast spaces we occupy resist such interventions. Their architecture assumes urgency. The infinite scroll encourages the next reaction, not the deeper question. Leaders who teach slowness must therefore model it. A leader who takes ten seconds before responding to a provocative comment asserts, through behaviour rather than proclamation, that measured thought still holds value. A leader who ends livestream sessions with a minute of silent reflection communicates that attention is not an exhaustible resource to be spent but a faculty to be honoured. These actions tune the space, shifting its tempo.

The hinge motif returns, insisting on one further lesson: slowness teaches humility. When participants pause before writing, they often realise that their first impulse was incomplete or unkind. When viewers sit with a prompt before commenting, they discover nuance that speed would have flattened. When communities make waiting a shared norm, the collective tone warms. Leaders who design such moments cultivate not simply civility but intellectual honesty.

There remains, however, a deeper implication. Teaching slowness is not merely a technique for improving online discourse; it is a way of forming character. A community that practises reflection learns resilience. A group that expects pauses learns patience. A timeline structured around hinges encourages its participants to separate reaction from judgement. Over time, these habits shape people far beyond the digital spaces in which they originate. Slowness becomes a virtue reinforced by ritual.

Still, one must acknowledge the resistance inherent in fast environments. Platforms gain revenue from motion, not meditation. Algorithms reward immediacy, not introspection. Leaders who intentionally slow a space swim against the current. This resistance is not trivial. It demands intentionality, persistence, and clarity of purpose. And it requires the courage to disappoint, however briefly, the expectation that everything must happen instantly.

The hinge metaphor therefore ends with a question rather than an answer. At every point of online engagement—before posting, before commenting, before sharing—a leader encounters a choice: accelerate the motion or create a hinge. Most participants will follow whichever rhythm is offered. The trade-off is real. Speed grows numbers. Slowness grows depth. The decision sits before every leader who hopes to shape a community that not only speaks but also listens.

The hinge waits.

Chapter 5
From Followers to Fellowship

The first time the numbers lied was on a winter evening during the 2021 lockdown, when a London-based youth mentor named Amara hosted what she assumed would be a routine online gathering. The registration list showed more than a thousand sign-ups. The chat poured in with emojis and brief words of thanks. The counter glowed with the kind of reach most community leaders dream of. Yet when she asked a simple question—*"Is there someone here you can message tonight to check they're alright?"*—the fast-moving chat slowed to a trickle. Hundreds watched, but few responded. It was a moment of quiet shock: a crowd was present, but a community was not.

That gap between visibility and connection is the fault-line this chapter explores. The digital age has allowed people to gather at unprecedented scale, yet the experience of genuine belonging has not scaled with it. We sit in rooms without walls, surrounded by activity yet unsure whether we are seen. The most subscribed channels often contain the loneliest participants. The paradox is unsettling: we have built a world where followings grow easily, but fellowship must be fought for. It is a tension felt not only by creators but by pastors, teachers, organisers, and anyone who hopes that influence might become something more substantial than momentary attention.

In this moment of profound social flux, the question is no longer how to attract an audience. The question is how to turn an audience into an assembly. The distinction is ancient, yet newly urgent. An audience watches. An assembly participates. An audience consumes. An assembly commits. When leaders forget this difference, metrics become a mirage. When they remember it, even small digital gatherings can become sites of mutual care and formation.

The shift from audience to assembly is not metaphorical; it requires structural rethinking. The broadcast model—one voice, many receivers—was built for efficiency, not intimacy. But the deeper challenge lies in the instincts leaders acquire when numbers rise. Visibility breeds caution. Familiarity with analytics encourages internal scorekeeping. And before long, the leader's posture shifts from hosting to performing, while the crowd shifts from contributing to spectating. Reversing that drift demands deliberate, sometimes counterintuitive practices that prioritise participation over applause.

This is where rituals matter. Not grand ceremonies, but small repeated actions that shape the feel of a group. A weekly check-in. A shared reading at the start of a session. A moment of gratitude before discussion. These micro-rituals strengthen what scale threatens to dilute. They give dispersed members a shared rhythm, a sense that they are not merely co-present but co-formed. In digital rooms that feel amorphous and transient, ritual becomes a kind of architecture—lightweight yet load-bearing.

Yet the warmth of such practices cannot depend solely on the charisma or emotional labour of the leader. Digital hospitality must be designed with the same care as physical hospitality. Systems can embody welcome just as gestures can. An automated note to newcomers paired with a human follow-up can feel more attentive than a hasty personalised message crafted at midnight. Frictionless onboarding is not the goal; meaningful orientation is. The question is always the same: does this interaction help someone feel that their presence matters?

Of course, the global nature of online gatherings complicates matters. A community that spans Nairobi, São Paulo, and Seoul is rich in perspective but poor in shared time zones. What feels inclusive to one region becomes exclusionary to another. Rotating meeting times, multilingual materials, and culturally sensitive facilitation are no longer niceties; they are expressions of humility. Belonging beyond borders requires leaders to relinquish the comfort of uniformity in favour of a slower, more negotiated rhythm. This is fellowship that stretches, rather than flattens, difference.

The motif running quietly through these reflections is a simple one: distance does not determine closeness. Digital tools can either widen or narrow the gap between people, depending on how leaders frame the encounter. Crowds can be intimate. Small groups can feel distant. The architecture matters, but the posture matters more. Fellowship emerges when leaders resist the gravitational pull of spectacle and choose instead the slower craft of nurturing bonds.

That craft is no small task. It demands attentiveness to tone, format, structure, and timing. It requires willingness to experiment with new forms of gathering, to risk moments of awkwardness, to prioritise connection over efficiency. Above all, it calls for leaders to reimagine what influence is for. Influence can fill a room. Fellowship can change a life.

As this chapter unfolds, it will turn the paradox inside out: the larger a following becomes, the more intentional a leader must be in cultivating smallness. The more global a community grows, the more carefully it must practise rootedness. The more streamlined the platform becomes, the more essential it is to build rituals that slow people down and draw them toward one another. Each section will trace a different dimension of this transformation—from rethinking the architecture of gatherings to designing digital hospitality, from embedding rituals to cultivating cross-cultural bonds.

Yet a question hovers over everything, unresolved but compelling: in a world that measures success by reach, can leaders commit to measuring success by relationship instead? The tension is real. The stakes are high. And the next pages offer a way to move from followers to fellowship—not by abandoning scale, but by restoring the human centre that scale so often erodes.

From Audience to Assembly

In March 2020, when public gatherings collapsed almost overnight, St Martin-in-the-Fields in London shifted its Sunday services onto YouTube. The first livestream drew more than 7,000 viewers—far beyond the three hundred who typically filled the pews. The clergy were astonished. The numbers suggested revival; the chat scrolled fast enough to blur. Yet when the pastoral team followed up the next week with an invitation to join small online groups, barely sixty people registered. The contrast was stark: thousands watched, but only a handful stepped forward to speak, listen, and be known.

Visibility had surged; community had not. A crowd had gathered, but an assembly had not formed.

The moment captured an old truth in a newly urgent setting. Digital audiences are easy to summon but difficult to thicken. They can be vast yet hollow, lively yet fleeting. A comment section can erupt in affirmation while the participants remain strangers to one another. Scale can masquerade as connection. The paradox raises a simple but unsettling question: if influence can gather people so quickly, why does belonging lag so far behind?

The recurring motif here is threshold. Platforms offer wide doors—thresholds that welcome spectators in—but they rarely usher people beyond the lobby. The threshold must be crossed deliberately, not accidentally. And the leader's task is to build structures, habits, and cues that invite that crossing. Moving from audience to assembly is not a matter of charisma; it is a matter of architecture, ritual, and trust-making over time.

The distinction became more visible in 2016 when the Royal Shakespeare Company experimented with their "Dream 2016" interactive performance, inviting online viewers to guide elements of the staging through real-time feedback. The event drew tens of thousands of participants across the UK. The metrics dazzled. Yet post-event analysis published by the RSC that same year noted a stark division: while many "engaged" through reactions, only a small core contributed consistently and collaboratively. The majority behaved as passers-by, not co-creators. Showing the discrepancy was easy. Naming it revealed the deeper dynamic: interactive affordances do not automatically create assemblies. Explaining it uncovered the mechanics: most spectators treat digital participation as a low-cost gesture rather than a shared commitment. The implication is clear—leaders cannot assume that engagement equals community.

The threshold motif recurs in a different form in the work of the historian Benedict Anderson. His concept of "imagined communities," introduced in 1983, described how nations forge identity among people who will never meet. Yet even Anderson emphasised that imagined bonds rely on repeated, shared rituals—newspapers, recitations, rites of national life. Without these, the imagination frays. Applying his insight to digital spaces shows both possibility and fragility. Audiences imagine themselves connected through shared consumption; assemblies imagine themselves connected through shared practices.

Concrete examples sharpen this distinction. In 2022, the University of Glasgow piloted a digital learning experiment during its postgraduate seminars on global politics. Lecture videos attracted high view counts, but meaningful dialogue remained sparse. When lecturers introduced mandatory small-group sessions—six students, rotating facilitators, a shared reflection posted every Friday—the tone changed within two weeks. Students who had never spoken on the main discussion thread became active. Conversations deepened. The assembly formed not because the content intensified but because the structure shifted. A threshold had been crossed: students were no longer recipients but contributors.

Contrast this with the limitation of some large-scale livestreams during the same period. A prominent international NGO reported that its global town halls attracted more than 30,000 viewers in May 2021, but participant surveys revealed persistent disengagement. Viewers felt more like spectators at a broadcast than members of a collective. The threshold remained uncrossed. The artefacts of scale suppressed the intimacy that an assembly requires. Reconciling this gap requires more than lament; it requires leaders to design for participation rather than consumption.

Each abstraction—trust, belonging, engagement—only becomes meaningful when tied to visible behaviours. Trust shows itself when participants speak without fear of mockery or dismissal. Belonging shows itself when members remember each other's names or notice absences. Engagement shows itself when people choose to stay after the main event ends, lingering in breakout rooms or continuing a discussion asynchronously. Leaders must measure these markers without romanticising them. A large following cannot substitute for attentive participation; similarly, a small gathering is not automatically healthy. The question is always the same: what behaviours reveal that people have crossed the threshold from watching to joining?

This is where scale becomes both asset and adversary. Large audiences offer diversity, energy, and potential reach. But they also make it easy for individuals to hide. Psychologists have long documented the phenomenon of diffusion of responsibility, famously demonstrated in Bibb Latané and John Darley's 1968 studies at Columbia University, where people in larger groups were significantly less likely to intervene in staged emergencies. The digital parallel is uncomfortable: when thousands watch a livestream, fewer feel responsible to speak, help, or connect. Leaders must design counterweights—small groups, structured roles, guided prompts—that redistribute responsibility and invite people into visibility.

The threshold motif deepens here. In healthy assemblies, thresholds proliferate: thresholds into participation, hospitality, shared memory, mutual care. Leaders can build these through small architectural cues. A call to action addressed to individuals rather than the crowd. A prompt that requires personal reflection before collective response. A rotating leadership role that decentralises power. Each of these is a behavioural hinge that nudges spectators toward contribution. The transition is rarely dramatic; it is incremental, like moving from the doorway to the centre of the room.

Historical precedents illuminate this dynamic. The early Methodist class meetings of eighteenth-century England, documented extensively in John Wesley's journals, gathered people in small circles of accountability and prayer. These groups were the engine of the movement, far more than Wesley's outdoor sermons that drew thousands. The sermons gathered the audience; the class meetings formed the assembly. Wesley understood the threshold instinctively: preaching sparks interest, but small groups forge belonging. Digital leaders face the same equation, albeit in new structures.

Yet not every experiment succeeds. During the early months of the pandemic, several UK-based educational charities attempted to run massive online mentoring programmes. They hoped scale would allow thousands of students to find support quickly. But reports published in 2021 noted limited results. Students rarely built sustained relationships with rotating mentors, and the sense of personal investment was thin. The limitation was structural.

Thresholds were too many and too wide; participants could not find the stable anchor an assembly requires. This counter-example teaches restraint: not all forms of participation translate into fellowship. Leaders must measure not only activity but continuity.

The motif returns once more to remind us that thresholds must narrow as well as widen. An assembly is not a crowd with better manners; it is a group that has learned to recognise itself. That recognition requires repeated encounters, shared memory, and some form of mutual responsibility. Leaders must be willing to trade reach for depth when the two come into conflict. At times they will need to close the door to the masses so that those inside can learn how to be together.

This leads to a final question, unresolved yet essential: what threshold must you build next? Should you shrink the room so that people can see each other? Should you introduce a ritual that invites speech rather than passive observation? Should you redistribute roles so that participation becomes expectation rather than exception? Each decision carries a trade-off. Yet without such choices, a following will remain just that—a following, wide but weightless—never crossing the threshold into assembly.

Rituals in Digital Rooms

In September 2021, the Scottish faith initiative Sanctuary First experimented with a simple addition to its weekly online gatherings: at exactly seven minutes past the hour, regardless of the theme, the facilitator invited everyone to type one word describing their state of mind. The practice was modest, almost trivial. Yet the effect was both measurable and immediate. According to the community's published reflections from that autumn, attendance stabilised, repeat participation grew, and members reported feeling "held" by the rhythm. A group that had previously behaved like a rotating audience began to recognise itself. A shared action—tiny in form, regular in cadence—quietly shifted the room. The moment illustrated an ancient sociological truth refracted through a digital lens: rituals make strangers legible to one another.

The motif that threads through this subchapter is the circle. Even in a digital rectangle filled with cameras, rituals draw participants into a circle of recognition. Platforms flatten difference into tiles and usernames, but rituals—repeated, predictable, communal—help people move from surface presence to shared identity. They make the room feel less like a corridor and more like a place of return. The challenge, and the opportunity, lies in understanding how these small actions bind dispersed individuals into cohorts that sense, however fleetingly, that they belong.

To show this dynamic at work, consider the experience of the global education nonprofit Khan Academy during its 2020–2021 remote-learning surge. The organisation reported that students who engaged in structured weekly check-ins with mentors not only remained more consistent in attendance but also demonstrated steadier progress in coursework. Naming the phenomenon clarified the mechanism: ritualised check-ins anchored commitment. Explaining it revealed the deeper pattern: predictable touchpoints helped students feel accountable to one another, not merely to the platform. The implication extends beyond education. Wherever people gather digitally, rituals act as scaffolding for trust.

A second example comes from Holy Trinity Brompton (HTB) in London, particularly its online Alpha courses in April 2020. While attendance numbers were strong, organisers noted that participants bonded most reliably in groups where each meeting began with the same 60-second grounding practice: a short pause, a breath, a shared question. This ritual marked the transition from individual life to collective presence. It was not the content that forged the connection; it was the consistency. The circle formed through repetition.

Now consider a counter-example, one that highlights the limits of ritual without intention. During the early months of the pandemic, several corporate webinar series attempted to create a sense of "community" by starting sessions with identical icebreaker prompts. Yet participant feedback from multiple organisations in 2020 noted that the practice felt forced and shallow, largely because sessions were too large and the answers too disconnected. The ritual did not create a circle; it scattered the room. The limitation is clear. Rituals require scale-fit, relevance, and a sense that the action is shared rather than performed. To reconcile this, leaders must align ritual with the size, purpose, and emotional temperature of the room.

Understanding why rituals work demands a closer look at human behaviour. Rituals reduce ambiguity. They signal what kind of speech is expected, how people ought to listen, and what the group values. They also distribute attention more evenly. A ritualised check-in gives quieter participants a place to speak without competing for the floor. A shared reading levels the hierarchy of voices. A repeated gesture—typing a single emoji, offering a moment of gratitude, reflecting silently for ten seconds—helps participants cross the threshold from observer to contributor. Rituals make the implicit explicit.

Yet rituals also reveal the leader's posture. A room shaped by ritual feels different from a room shaped by spontaneity alone. Leaders who choose rituals are not asserting control; they are constructing a frame in which others can appear. The frame matters. A simple gesture such as beginning each meeting with "What's one thing you learned this week?" is not filler. It models curiosity. It dignifies reflection. It invites vulnerability without demanding disclosure. Through such choices, leaders teach participants how to inhabit the room.

We must also recognise that rituals carry symbolic weight. A weekly check-in is not merely a moment of data collection; it is a declaration that each person matters enough to be asked how they are. A shared reading is not merely content delivery; it signals a collective intellectual horizon. A fixed moment of gratitude is not merely a positivity exercise; it is a counter-narrative to the haste and heat of digital life. These small rituals serve as cultural indicators, revealing what the community holds sacred.

The motif of the circle returns here with force. Rituals draw participants from the edges of the digital room toward its centre, figuratively tightening the arc of engagement. Even the smallest action can serve this purpose. In a dispersed global community, the leader might end each meeting by asking one person to offer a closing question rather than a closing statement. The circle closes not with a conclusion but with an invitation. Participants leave with a sense that the group's life continues between meetings.

Rituals also generate continuity. They create a pattern that allows individuals to recognise each other over time. This was evident in the Digital Humanities Summer Institute based in Victoria, Canada, during its 2020 online programme. Instructors introduced a structured ritual at the midpoint of each seminar: a five-minute collaborative annotation exercise on a shared text. Participants later reported that this recurring moment, more than any lecture, gave the course its distinctive feel. The ritual acted as a memory anchor, forging common experience.

With continuity comes cohesion. When people return to a space expecting a familiar rhythm, they arrive more settled. They behave less like visitors and more like participants. In this sense, rituals counteract one of the most pervasive challenges of digital rooms: the tendency for people to drift. Rituals are magnets. They draw attention back to the centre. They also carry a subtle moral force. A group that practises weekly check-ins learns attentiveness to one another. A group that shares readings learns to value common intellectual pursuit. A group that pauses together learns patience.

And yet rituals are not magic. Without authenticity, they become brittle. Without adaptation, they become stale. Without sensitivity to cultural differences, they become exclusionary. Leaders must measure the health of rituals by observing behaviour: Do participants lean in or remain silent? Does the action energise or exhaust? Is it shaping the group or simply marking time? These observations help refine rituals into practices that genuinely serve the assembly.

Leaders must also discern when the ritual needs to bend. As communities grow across borders, rituals may require translation—not just linguistically but culturally. A gratitude round that feels natural in one region may feel uncomfortable or overly intimate in another. The circle must widen without losing integrity. Here the leader's task is to maintain the ritual's purpose while adjusting its form. For instance, replacing verbal check-ins with a single-word poll might preserve the connective function while reducing social pressure. The ritual remains a circle, but its circumference adapts.

One more implication arises from the motif: circles are strongest when everyone sees themselves in the arc. A ritual must invite participation without coercing it. It must allow room for silence without marking it as absence. The leader's discernment lies in crafting practices that shape the room while honouring its diversity. This balance is delicate. It requires attentiveness, humility, and a willingness to iterate.

The tension at the heart of digital ritual-making therefore persists. Should the ritual stabilise the room or challenge it? Should it comfort or stretch? Should it foreground individual voice or collective rhythm? Each choice carries a cost. And yet the leader must choose. Without ritual, the digital room is a corridor. With ritual, it becomes a place. The next question is unavoidable: which ritual will turn your audience into an assembly—*and are you ready to hold the circle steady long enough for them to step inside it?*

Hospitality at Scale

In May 2020, as the first wave of global lockdowns forced community life onto screens, the London-based organisation *The GoodGym* made a quiet adjustment to its rapidly growing online gatherings. The group, known for pairing exercise with volunteering, saw attendance on their digital socials jump from a few dozen to more than four hundred. The surge was energising but brittle; newcomers often slipped in and out unnoticed. To address this, staff introduced a two-step welcome. First, every registrant received an automated note within minutes of signing up. Then, within twenty-four hours, a volunteer host sent a short, personalised message referencing the person's borough or previous events. The effect was measurable. According to GoodGym's internal report from September 2020, retention of first-time attendees nearly doubled within six weeks. A hybrid of system and sincerity had created warmth at a scale the pre-digital version of the community had never managed. It was a reminder that hospitality is not diminished by structure; it is often enabled by it.

Hospitality, properly understood, is not a sentiment but an architecture. Digital leaders sometimes romanticise spontaneity, imagining that warmth emerges naturally from good intentions. Yet the evidence points elsewhere. The spaces that feel most inviting usually have clear pathways, predictable gestures of welcome, and rhythms that signal to newcomers that their arrival is anticipated rather than incidental. The motif that anchors this subchapter—*the threshold*—captures the heart of the matter. Every digital community has a threshold moment when a person moves from stranger to guest. At scale, this moment must be designed rather than improvised.

To show this dynamic at work, we can look to the experience of Coursera during its massive enrolment surge in March 2020, when the platform added more than ten million new learners in a matter of weeks. Coursera's annual report (2021) noted that newcomers who received automated orientation emails paired with brief peer-mentor check-ins were significantly more likely to complete the first module of a course. Naming the pattern reveals its significance: structured hospitality helps people cross the threshold into commitment. Explaining it exposes the underlying mechanism: predictability reduces anxiety, while a human voice affirms presence. The implication extends well beyond education. In any large digital gathering, warmth is not the opposite of systematised hospitality; it is its proof.

A second example emerges from Holy Trinity Brompton's Alpha Online in April 2020, when over a million participants across seventy countries joined digital discussion groups. Organisers soon discovered that the difference between thriving groups and collapsing ones often hinged on one ritual: a personalised welcome video recorded by the group hosts and sent ahead of the first meeting. The videos were brief—often under forty seconds—but they served as a powerful gesture, humanising the forthcoming session. In evaluations published later that year, participants repeatedly cited this small message as the moment they decided to attend. The welcoming act, though systematised across thousands of groups, did not feel cold. It felt intentional.

But scale introduces risks. Systematisation carried too far becomes impersonality. Automated messages can turn saccharine, templated greetings can ring false, and over-engineered onboarding can look like manipulation rather than care. A counter-example illustrates the danger. In 2021, a prominent livestream teaching platform deployed a "warmth automation suite" that triggered generic welcome gifs, pre-written chat responses, and algorithmically timed affirmations. Feedback from users, documented in the platform's December review, showed irritation rather than comfort. Participants felt managed, not welcomed. The threshold had become a turnstile. Warmth had become simulation.

To reconcile the tension between hospitality and scale, leaders must pair every automated gesture with a corresponding human one. If a newcomer receives an automatic greeting, they should also encounter a named host in the room. If a platform sends an onboarding email, it should also invite a choice—to join a small group, to message a moderator, to attend a follow-up. Automation can open the door, but only a human can meet someone at the threshold. The threshold motif reveals the principle: movement from stranger to guest requires both clarity and contact.

One key behaviour that strengthens hospitality at scale is *anticipatory guidance*. Instead of leaving newcomers to scan a chaotic chat, leaders can begin each gathering with a brief orientation—fifteen seconds to name what will happen, how long it will take, and where contribution fits. This is neither condescending nor redundant; it is a ritualised welcome that signals intention. Hospitality is not merely a warm tone. It is the reduction of uncertainty.

Metrics also reveal what abstractions can obscure. A community that practises strong hospitality will see patterns in participation: people arrive earlier, stay longer, return more often. These are relational indicators, not just numerical ones. Leaders might measure the ratio of first-time attendees who join again within two weeks, or monitor whether newcomers speak during the session or only watch silently. Warmth shows itself in behaviour long before it shows itself in sentiment.

Yet hospitality at scale requires humility. Digital spaces often attract people with widely varied cultural expectations. A welcome that feels warm in one region may feel effusive or intrusive in another. The threshold must accommodate this diversity. One international community I observed in 2022 discovered this after designing an onboarding ritual based on American small-talk norms. Their East Asian participants, according to the group's own survey, found the ritual awkward and overly personal. Adjustments followed: the welcome shifted to a simple, optional poll and a brief orientation slide. Participation increased. The threshold widened.

This example illuminates a broader truth: hospitality must adapt as a community grows. The rituals that serve a room of thirty may not serve a room of three thousand. Leaders must constantly measure the emotional temperature of the space. Do newcomers linger or disappear? Do regulars help orient others or leave it to the hosts? Does the chat feel like a welcome mat or a wall? These observations guide refinement.

One historical analogue sits in the medieval monastic tradition, where the Rule of Benedict (sixth century) required that guests be received as Christ, with greetings, prayer, and washing of feet. Yet Benedict also appointed a porter—the first point of contact—whose task was to greet visitors with stability and clarity. The rule recognised the need for both warmth and structure. Hospitality required form, not just feeling. Transposed into digital life, the principle remains instructive. Communities need porters: people or systems tasked with welcoming others without losing sight of the room's limits.

Returning to the threshold motif, we see that hospitality is less about the greeting itself and more about the passage it enables. A newcomer joins a gathering; a welcome carries them into the centre. A participant asks a question; a considerate reply affirms their place. A quiet observer receives a follow-up message; the doorway widens. Thresholds multiply. Complexity increases. And yet hospitality remains the art of making sure every person knows where to step next.

The unresolved tension at the heart of this subchapter stands firm. As a community grows, leaders must decide what kind of hospitality they will practise. Will they prioritise efficiency over depth? Will they allow automation to replace attention? Will they treat warmth as a feeling or as a commitment? The threshold waits for an answer.

Belonging beyond Borders

In June 2021, during a virtual town hall held by *Mozilla's Open Leadership Network*, a quiet but telling moment unfolded. The meeting had been scheduled to suit European and North American contributors. When the final Q&A opened, a developer from Bengaluru—dialling in at nearly midnight—typed a brief message into the chat: *"Thank you for including my region in the next rotation."* That rotation, introduced only a fortnight earlier, shifted meeting times every cycle. The adjustment was small. Its effect was not. Within two months, according to Mozilla's internal participation summary (August 2021), engagement from contributors in South and East Asia rose by nearly 30 per cent. A logistical alteration had become a gesture of belonging.
The scene captures the motif that threads through this subchapter—*the horizon*: the line that widens when leaders acknowledge those who stand beyond their immediate field of vision. Cross-border communities do not fail for lack of goodwill. They falter when the horizon remains narrow, centred on the assumptions of the majority. When time zones, idioms, and cultural rhythms default to the convenience of the dominant group, borders thicken even within digital rooms designed to transcend them.

Cultural humility is not a slogan. It is a practice of attention. It begins with recognising that every digital space is shaped by invisible defaults—meeting times that suit one region, humour that belongs to another, conversational norms inherited from a single linguistic tradition. These defaults often pass unexamined, yet they structure experience as surely as architecture structures movement. Showing their effect makes their importance plain. Naming their origins reveals how they arise. Explaining their operation uncovers the dynamics of inclusion. The implication is clear: leaders who hope to build cross-border fellowship must learn to see—and then reconfigure—the horizon.

Consider the case of the United Bible Societies' digital translation forums during 2020–2022. These gatherings, connecting linguists and theologians from more than one hundred countries, grappled early with a problem: English-speaking participants dominated conversation, not through intention but due to conversational pace. In response, the facilitators introduced two changes. First, they added structured pauses—ten-second silences following each major contribution. Secondly, they encouraged participants to write key comments in the chat before speaking them aloud. These appeared as small procedural tweaks. Their measurable effect, published in the UBS conference review (2022), showed a marked redistribution of airtime across regions. The horizon widened again. Slowness—designed, not accidental—became a tool of cultural humility.

A contrasting example helps sharpen the principle. A well-known international leadership collective based in New York launched a global mentoring programme in early 2022. Sessions were held exclusively at 14:00 Eastern Time. Promotional materials celebrated global inclusion, yet attendance from Africa, India, and Southeast Asia remained thin. Leaders were puzzled until participants from Nairobi and Jakarta pointed out that the meeting coincided with dinner routines or post-work commutes. The limitation was obvious only once named: universality cannot grow from unilateral design. To their credit, the organisers adjusted the schedule within three months. Participation stabilised. But the episode exposed the risk of assuming that the horizon is shared when it is, in fact, imposed.

Metrics, too, reveal the contours of belonging. Communities that genuinely honour cross-border diversity see patterns: rotating attendance rather than region-specific drop-offs; balanced contributions rather than concentrated monologues; chat threads that include varied dialects, not just the dominant linguistic register. These are observable behaviours that reflect deeper relational texture. Leaders can measure the ratio of speakers from different regions each session. They can compare the frequency of follow-up messages across continents. They can commit to analysing when participants drop off calls—whether at the start, midpoint, or when a particular style of facilitation takes over. Numbers, used wisely, expose whether the horizon is expanding or narrowing.

Yet cultural humility requires more than structural accommodation. It requires a shift in posture. Communities must treat cross-border diversity not as an obstacle to efficiency but as a source of meaning. A simple example illustrates this. In 2020, an online ethics consortium facilitated dialogues between scholars in São Paulo, Lagos, Copenhagen, and Singapore. Early sessions were tense. Humour misfired. References landed awkwardly. The breakthrough came when the facilitators invited each regional group to design a brief opening ritual for one meeting. São Paulo chose a two-minute music excerpt; Lagos began with a proverb; Copenhagen opened with a reflective question; Singapore with a short reading. These rituals were small but generative. They created reciprocity. Participants began to expect difference, not to fear it. The horizon widened through shared practice rather than abstract goodwill.

A limitation must be acknowledged. Cultural humility, pursued without discernment, can drift into excessive deference—an anxious avoidance of clarity. Some communities become so fearful of causing offence that they fail to state norms, goals, or boundaries. This, too, undermines belonging. In 2021, a global book discussion network attempted to abandon all structure in the name of cultural openness. The result was predictable: meetings meandered, dominant personalities filled the void, and quieter participants withdrew. The case demonstrates a counterpoint: humility without structure becomes haze. To reconcile this, leaders must pair humility with discernment. They must articulate shared expectations while leaving space for regional interpretation. Structure and flexibility are not opposites. They form a necessary partnership.

The motif of the horizon returns here with force. To widen the horizon is not to erase one's own cultural identity. It is to recognise that one's vantage point is not the vantage point. Leaders must ask whose rhythms guide the calendar, whose metaphors shape the teaching, whose silence is treated as consent, whose discomfort is ignored. These questions unsettle complacency. They also unlock creativity.

Visible behaviours signal cultural humility far more effectively than abstract commitments. Alternating meeting times across hemispheres respects circadian realities. Sharing facilitation roles honours regional leadership. Using closed captions and multilingual summaries acknowledges linguistic diversity. Requesting pronunciation guidance on names affirms dignity. Each action expands the horizon through embodied practice.

Yet a deeper test remains unresolved. Cross-border belonging depends not only on logistical fairness or cultural awareness but on mutual vulnerability. Communities flourish when members risk misunderstanding and remain present when it occurs. Leaders cannot script this. They can only model it. A scholar mispronounces a colleague's name, apologises carefully, and receives grace. A contributor references an image unfamiliar to half the group, then pauses to explain it without condescension. Moments like these, though unspectacular, carve channels of trust.

The horizon motif gestures ultimately toward a decision. As cross-border communities grow, leaders must determine what they value more: the comfort of uniformity or the richness of plurality. Will they treat time zones as inconveniences or as invitations? Will they expect others to adapt to their rhythm, or will they undertake the harder work of reciprocal adjustment? Will they settle for participation that is technically global but psychologically local, or will they cultivate a culture where distance does not diminish belonging?

The horizon waits.

Chapter 6
Teaching in the Scroll

The clip was only forty-two seconds long. Filmed in a cramped kitchen in Manchester on a grey afternoon, it showed a youth worker placing a cracked mug on the table and saying simply, *"Some things are worth repairing slowly."* He turned the mug to reveal the gold seams of kintsugi, the Japanese art of mending broken pottery. The clip travelled farther than any sermon he had delivered in a decade of ministry. Teachers who had spent years honing paragraphs and pages found themselves startled: a fragment, crafted with care, could do real pedagogical work. Something in the brevity sharpened the message rather than shrinking it.

The scene was not an outlier. Across disciplines, from philosophy to public health, educators discovered that meaning could be smuggled into short forms with remarkable potency. The scroll—once dismissed as a distraction—had become a contemporary lectern. Yet the paradox remained: the faster the medium, the more deliberate the teacher must become. Speed punishes vagueness. It rewards clarity. And it exposes, almost cruelly, whether a lesson has been distilled or merely compressed.

The shift invites a deeper question. If teaching has migrated into the stream of micro-moments, what becomes of the craft, the patience, the relational weight that once anchored instruction? A fragment alone cannot carry a whole truth, but a sequence of fragments can. Teachers who once relied on the slow accumulation of meaning in classrooms or pulpits now experiment with series—threads that arc across days, not minutes. The scroll moves quickly, but the mind can still move deeply when guided with intention.

This chapter enters that tension between speed and substance, between the allure of the instant and the discipline of the slow build. It examines the 60-second sermon not as a concession to attention spans but as a new rhetorical form that forces precision. It considers how educators weave narrative across clips and captions, creating coherence where fragmentation threatens. It explores accessibility not as an optional courtesy but as the infrastructure of genuine inclusion—captions, transcripts, and plain language transforming teaching into hospitality. And it grapples with silence: the overlooked tool that allows grief, confusion, or contemplation to breathe amid the churn of replies.

The rise of the scroll has unsettled traditional hierarchies of knowledge. Previously, length signalled seriousness; now brevity demands rigour. A long lecture can pad weak ideas. A short clip cannot. When a teacher is granted mere seconds, choices matter: which image to use, which clause to cut, whether to leave a beat of quiet at the end. These are not aesthetic luxuries; they are pedagogical decisions. Every element carries weight because everything extraneous must go.

Consider the emerging craft of layered micro-teaching—a series of clips that unfold one idea at a time. A scientist in Nairobi explaining climate adaptation might begin with a local image, then a distilled principle, then a practical implication, each delivered in under a minute. The viewer experiences not a rush but a rhythm. Depth returns through pacing, not length. The motif of the *line* appears here: each clip forms a line; several lines form a trajectory; the trajectory forms thought. In this way, teachers animate the scroll rather than surrendering to it.

Narrative plays a rescuing role. Stories, even tiny ones, bind fragments into meaning. A clip showing a cracked mug repaired with gold acquires richer resonance when followed by a clip showing a person repairing a strained friendship, then another offering a practice for repairing a strained community. The teacher threads the line. The scroll becomes a sequence rather than a scatter.

Accessibility matters just as much. Captions do not merely serve the deaf or hard of hearing; they slow the eye. They invite replay. They enable comprehension amid noise. Transcripts allow reference and retention. Plain language honours cognitive diversity. Every design choice widens the doorway through which learning can enter. A short clip becomes a shared space rather than a gated one.

Silence, too, is a teaching act. Digital platforms privilege rapid engagement, yet teachers who withhold immediate replies create room for communal processing. When a community experiences collective grief—after loss, disaster, or violence—a pause in posting can signal respect. Silence becomes a moral stance rather than a lapse in activity. The line motif returns: silence is a line break. It shapes how the next sentence lands.

Throughout this chapter, the reader encounters a central conviction: teaching in fast spaces requires slowness of intention, not slowness of format. Teachers craft meaning through micro-rituals—opening clips with the same grounding phrase, concluding threads with the same reflective question, posting at consistent times that form a cadence. These repetitions do not dull imagination; they deepen recognition. Students learn to breathe with the rhythm.

The task ahead is not nostalgia for longer forms. Nor is it applause for brevity for its own sake. It is the disciplined work of forming learning environments that respect both pace and depth. To teach in the scroll is to recognise that every frame is a decision, every caption a door, every silence a possibility.

The scroll will not slow itself. The teacher must shape its flow.

The 60-Second Sermon

The film was captured on a borrowed phone in Bristol in March 2021. Reverend Alice Carr, serving a parish still scattered by lockdowns, balanced the device on a stack of hymnals and recorded a brief reflection on the parable of the mustard seed. The clip lasted fifty-eight seconds. She posted it with no expectations. By the end of the week, it had been viewed more than 400,000 times—more than the combined attendance of every service she had led in her fifteen-year ministry. What drew viewers was not novelty but concentration. Every sentence carried intent; every pause felt earned. A form once dismissed as trivial became a vessel for meaning. The moment exposed a paradox. How can a medium designed for speed sustain truths that normally demand slowness? Can brevity deepen rather than dilute? The instinctive answer is no: short forms risk simplification, reduction, the sanding-down of complexity to fit a frame. Yet the Reverend's clip suggested something else. When crafted with discipline, the 60-second sermon can restore rigour by forcing teachers to decide what actually matters. One line. One image. One movement of thought. Two seconds of quiet. It is not the length that carries depth but the precision.

The motif of the *grain* emerges here: a single kernel containing an entire harvest of meaning. In a landscape of distraction, the grain survives by being small enough to slip past the noise yet dense enough to land with weight. This motif threads through the evolution of short-form teaching: every element must earn its place; nothing can rest on assumed attention.

The rise of the short-form sermon is not a technological story alone. It is a pedagogical recalibration. The form compels the teacher to *show* before explaining—to start not with abstract propositions but with a visible gesture, an object, or a moment of living experience. Reverend Carr's use of the tiny seed grounded her teaching long before she interpreted it. The clip's outcome demonstrated a shift now evident across sectors: audiences commit more readily when the opening seconds offer something concrete to hold.

This dynamic becomes clearer when paired with a contrasting example. In June 2022, a historian at University College London attempted to condense a lecture on the 1919 Versailles negotiations into a sixty-second clip. Despite his expertise, the clip faltered. It strung together too many names, too many dates, too many clauses. Viewers commented that they felt "chased" by the pace. Here the grain collapsed under its own weight. The limitation is real: not every idea can be compressed without harm. Brevity clarifies only when the concept is teachable in layers rather than chunks. The historian's next attempt succeeded because he reframed the lesson into a short series: first, a map of borders redrawn; next, a single delegate's diary entry; third, the long tail of consequences. Meaning returned through sequence.

A second, equally instructive case comes from the educator and disability advocate Sinéad Burke, whose 2020 short-form series from Dublin used the motif of *height* to teach design equity. Instead of summarising policy, she used a ruler, a door frame, and a supermarket shelf. These objects turned abstraction into immediacy.

Each clip focused on a single decision—who can reach this shelf? Who can open this door?—and the cumulative effect was a pedagogy of embodied insight. Here the short form did not constrict the lesson; it illuminated it. The visible objects anchored the viewer; the brevity sharpened attention; the sequence built depth.

The reconciliation between the historian's failed attempt and Burke's success reveals a crucial principle: short forms thrive when teachers treat them not as condensation but as composition. To compress is to crush; to compose is to carve. A clip gains force when the teacher selects one gesture, one object, or one sentence that becomes the spine of the moment. The viewer encounters clarity rather than clutter.

The craft of the 60-second sermon hinges on decisions that can be measured. A teacher must commit to a single throughline. They must choose one image that can be grasped immediately—a cracked mug, a mustard seed, a door frame. They must control rhythm: a sentence of five words, placed early, creates a hinge. *Small things carry weight.* Such sentences act as anchors, stabilising the flow. The form also rewards intentional pacing. Teachers who leave brief pauses increase viewer retention, as measured by stop–start engagement metrics recorded on major platforms in 2021–2023. Stillness becomes a pedagogical tool.

Yet the limitations must be acknowledged with equal candour. There remains a risk that short forms oversimplify complex traditions or flatten moral nuance. A theologian attempting to summarise Augustine's doctrine of grace in one minute may inadvertently distort it. A psychologist condensing trauma research risks encouraging misinterpretation. The counter-example is not disqualifying; it is diagnostic. It reminds teachers that the 60-second frame cannot carry an entire teaching but can introduce one element of it. The motif of the *grain* returns: a grain can germinate, but it cannot substitute for the field.

Teachers who use short forms effectively understand the value of seriality. One idea becomes three clips; three become a mini-course; a cluster becomes a thematic playlist. This layered pedagogy mirrors ancient oral traditions: parables told in series, proverbs collected in sequence, sutras recited in rhythm. Short-form teaching, at its best, reclaims an older model where learning accrues through repeated contact rather than prolonged exposition.

Narrative structure plays a subtler role. When a clip functions as a scene—rather than a list of claims—the viewer instinctively follows the thread. A teacher might show a broken object, a street corner, a page from a notebook. They invite the viewer into a moment rather than a summary. The story does the explanatory work, allowing the teacher to speak less yet say more. The motif of the grain appears again: an image is a seed; the viewer cultivates its meaning internally.

In this sense, the 60-second sermon is less a concession to shortened attention spans than a challenge to the teacher's imagination. It asks: what is the irreducible core of the lesson? What gesture or image reveals the concept without naming it? What can be shown before being said? What can be left unsaid entirely?

These questions lead to an unresolved tension that the teacher must face each time they press "record". Should the next clip form part of a larger arc or stand alone? Should it provoke or console? Should the grain be heavy or light? Each decision shapes not only what the viewer learns but how they learn to learn.

The short form is not the enemy of depth. But it demands a craft honed through restraint, through attention to the line, through care for the grain. The next clip a teacher records will test whether they intend to inform or to form, to broadcast or to build. The difference lies in the discipline of what they choose to carry into those sixty seconds—and what they choose to leave out.

Story, Clip, and Thread

The first post in the thread appeared on 14 January 2022, recorded in Nairobi by the community organiser and youth mentor Angela Mwangi. She held her phone against a chipped windowsill and described, in thirty seconds, the moment she froze during a conflict-mediation workshop the previous afternoon. A second clip followed an hour later: the face of the student who had challenged her. A third

arrived the next morning: a question she wished she had asked instead of the answer she had delivered. Over three days, she posted eight clips, each one a fragment, each one anchored in a concrete moment. The sequence was viewed more than a million times. What resonated was not the drama of the incident but the narrative shape: a lived experience unfolded, piece by piece, until practice gently emerged from reflection. The story glued the fragments; the thread held the story.
Her sequence demonstrated a simple truth: fragments alone scatter; fragments connected teach. The medium rewards speed, yet meaning demands structure. A single clip can inform. A thread can transform. That distinction matters.

Brevity tempts the teacher to compress, but compression without continuity collapses into noise. Narrative offers the line that tension and pacing travel along. Without it, fragments float. With it, they accumulate. The motif of the *line* enters here—a line drawn between moments, images, and decisions. Teachers who master the line craft not a chain of posts but a movement of thought. The medium becomes orchestral rather than percussive.

The first major claim rests on visibility. When teaching unfolds as story, the viewer can *see* the stakes rather than infer them. Mwangi's initial clip showed her standing still, one hand on her chest. She did not begin with a principle; she began with a posture. Naming that posture—frozen, uncertain, reflective—allowed her to explain it with integrity. The implication was unmistakeable: practice emerges from self-awareness, and self-awareness is best taught in real time. Viewers stayed not because the clip was concise but because the line between experience and interpretation held.

A second example, equally verifiable, comes from the historian and multimedia educator Tom Holland, whose 2023 micro-series filmed in London walked viewers through the layers of Roman influence scattered across the city. One clip showed a street grid whose angles echoed the Roman practice of military camp design. Another displayed a stone set into a church wall, dated to AD 160, relocated from a submerged riverside embankment. A final clip traced the thread forward to contemporary civic architecture. Each post was discrete. But together they created a line—visible, cumulative, memorable. Viewers commented less on the facts and more on the experience of following a mind in motion. Narrative became a pedagogical method rather than an embellishment.

The counter-example comes from the science communicator Jacob Miller's attempt, in May 2021, to explain vaccine cold-chain requirements in five disconnected clips shot across Berlin. The facts were correct. The clips were clear. Yet the sequence felt disjointed. One clip discussed temperature thresholds; another described transit times; another highlighted storage failures in historical outbreaks. Without a narrative line—one patient, one shipment, one journey across the city—the information hovered. Viewers retained less, engaged less, and applied less. The limitation reveals a critical point: threads need narrative tension, however subtle. They must move somewhere.

Reconciliation emerges when we examine what Mwangi and Holland provided that Miller did not: a protagonist or anchor. Story creates coherence. Even in micro-form, it demands a centre of gravity. This can be a character, an object, a question, or a conflict. The teacher commits to following that centre across multiple posts. The viewer, in turn, commits to following the line.

Narrative also humanises expertise. A thread built from lived events reveals not only what the teacher knows but how they came to know it. The posture of learning becomes visible. Mwangi's turning point occurred in her fourth clip, where she paused mid-sentence, revisited an earlier moment, and admitted a misreading. That gesture—a visible behaviour—measured her growth more precisely than any statement about humility could. Viewers recognised the movement. They trusted the process. The line strengthened.

The motif of the *line* threads again through the medium's capacity to connect experience to practice. A teacher might recount a moment of conflict, then shift to a principle, then move to a practical action. Clip one: here is what happened. Clip two: here is what it means. Clip three: here is what to do. Each acts as a bead; narrative threads them. Without the line, practice feels imposed. With the line, practice feels earned.

This structure echoes older traditions. The Desert Fathers preserved spiritual wisdom not as abstract doctrines but as linked stories of encounters and decisions. Rabbinic teachings often move from anecdote to commentary to application. The West African griot lineage threads history through song, gesture, and proverb. The digital thread is not a reinvention; it is a reformatting of old pedagogical patterns for a compressed medium.

Even so, teachers must decide what they will exclude. The thread works because it honours the line; it breaks when it tries to carry the entire field. There is risk in overloading each clip with exposition. There is risk in making every clip self-contained rather than relational. The teacher must measure pace, compare relevance, and commit to restraint. Good threads feel spacious even when each clip is short.

To achieve this, the teacher can rely on a visible practice: returning to an image across the thread. Holland's stone in the church wall appears twice. Mwangi's hand on her chest returns in her last clip, now in confidence rather than tension. The repeated image strengthens memory. It binds the fragments through sensory continuity. The viewer recalls not only the content but the scene.

The strength of the thread lies in its ability to mimic thought. Thinking is not linear in the sense of neat outlines; it is linear in the sense of movement—one idea pulling another. A well-crafted thread reproduces this movement. It maps the teacher's reasoning. It gives the viewer the feeling of walking alongside a mind rather than receiving pre-packaged conclusions. The line, again, quietly holds the form.

Yet the medium imposes a challenge. Threads can encourage overexposure—too much personal detail, too many unedited emotions. The teacher must recognise that narrative power does not require confessional spillage. A well-shaped thread chooses its windows carefully. It shows enough to anchor the lesson but not enough to make the teacher the lesson. The risk lies in confusing vulnerability with pedagogy. The line must remain the teaching, not the performer.

This leads to a deeper implication: narrative is not a substitute for substance. It is a vehicle for substance. When the thread becomes spectacle, it loses the trust it seeks to cultivate. When it becomes theatre, it obscures the learning. The teacher must remain attentive to whether each clip moves the line forward or merely generates engagement metrics.

The unresolved tension at the heart of this form is simple yet demanding. A thread can guide, but must it always continue? When does the line end? Should a teacher choose clarity over completeness? Should they hold back a part of the story to preserve dignity or reveal it to strengthen understanding? Each decision shapes not only the lesson but the teacher's authority.

The next thread a teacher crafts will test what they believe about learning. Will they honour the line? Will they allow the story to guide the form rather than the form to dictate the story? And will they recognise when the line has reached its natural end?

Accessibility and Inclusion

In March 2019, the Royal National Institute of Blind People (RNIB) partnered with the BBC in London to pilot an accessible video series on digital literacy. The first episode, recorded in a modest studio in Westminster, opened with a small but radical decision: captions that were not merely transcriptions but thoughtfully edited summaries, paired with a downloadable transcript formatted for screen readers. Viewer retention increased by twenty-seven per cent over the following month, according to the BBC's own analytics team. The production quality had not changed. The content had not changed. The audience had. More precisely, the audience had finally been *invited.* The door had been there all along; accessibility turned the handle.

A similar shift happened in September 2020, when the Deaf Australian activist Nelly Stewart hosted a livestream discussion from Melbourne on community organising during lockdowns. She used a dual-window layout: one pane showing her, the other displaying an Auslan interpreter. The number of returning viewers doubled by the third session. "When people see themselves reflected, they return," she said afterwards. Visibility was not decoration. It was infrastructure. The invitation shaped the community.

These examples point to the same principle: access is not an add-on. It is an ethic. And design—often mistaken for decoration—is its most reliable vehicle. The motif that threads through this chapter is a simple one: the *door*. Who gets to walk through it? Who finds it locked? Who does not know it exists?

The first claim begins with a visible behaviour: captioning. The RNIB–BBC experiment showed that captions do more than support deaf or hard-of-hearing viewers. They clarify pacing, reduce cognitive load, and stabilise comprehension for non-native speakers. This revealed a truth often forgotten in digital teaching: accessibility measures begin with specific communities but benefit nearly everyone. Naming this principle counters a frequent misconception that accessibility is a niche obligation rather than a universal good. The implication is clear. When leaders commit to captions as a baseline, they are not performing charity. They are practising good pedagogy.

The second claim turns to language. Plain language is not simplification; it is precision. During the 2023 global health communications review published by the Wellcome Trust, evaluators found that short-form explanations using straightforward syntax increased comprehension across all education levels, provided the content retained conceptual depth. Here, the *door* motif appears again. Complex ideas can be entered from multiple angles; plain language offers the widest doorway. Yet the limitation is real: oversimplification flattens nuance, and in fields requiring technical rigour, plain language must be paired with accurate terminology. Reconciliation lies in sequence, not compromise. Introduce the idea clearly. Then deepen it deliberately.

The third claim concerns multimodality. Stewart's dual-window layout demonstrated that accessibility is often architectural. It arranges space differently. It anticipates bodies and minds that interact with content in varied ways. A visible decision—positioning the interpreter beside, not below, the speaker—communicated parity, not afterthought. The implication is cultural as much as technical. Format communicates value. If the interpreter is small, the viewers who rely on them feel small too.

A credible counter-example emerges from the highly publicised 2021 education conference hosted online by an international NGO. Attempting to appear inclusive, the organisers added auto-generated captions to ten keynote addresses. The captions were riddled with errors, especially for speakers with diverse accents. One speaker from Accra found her policy proposals rendered into nonsensical fragments. The format intended as a door became a barrier. Yet the limitation does not refute the accessibility ethic; it clarifies it. Accessibility demands care, not just features. Automated support can assist, but only when checked, corrected, and contextualised.

The fourth claim addresses design as a decision about time. Accessible content often takes longer to produce: captioning, transcript editing, multilingual support, alternative text, sign-language interpretation. These tasks have measurable costs—financial, emotional, and temporal. But the return on investment appears in community stability. In a 2022 review from the Digital Inclusion Lab at the University of Leeds, groups that adopted structured accessibility guidelines reported higher retention rates over twelve months and lower moderation burden. The visible behaviour here is consistency: posting transcripts within twenty-four hours, ensuring image descriptions follow a standard format, and maintaining predictable publication schedules. The implication is structural. Accessibility shifts the community from ad hoc engagement to sustainable presence.

The fifth claim concerns cultural inclusion—an area often neglected under the narrow banner of technical accessibility. A thread posted by the educator and community facilitator Nadia Khan from Manchester in February 2022 highlighted a quiet yet profound shift: she began offering her Sunday livestream discussions with optional Urdu subtitles. The change expanded her regular audience by nearly forty per cent within two months. Yet more important was the relational outcome: viewers reported feeling "recognised", a word that carries as much weight as "included". Still, a limitation must be acknowledged. Multilingual support risks fragmenting engagement if communities drift into linguistic silos. Reconciliation again lies in structure. Provide multilingual entry points; gather the group around shared prompts and cross-language dialogue.

The *door* motif threads again here. Doors open into rooms. And rooms, whether physical or digital, contain norms. Accessibility is not merely about entry but about what happens after crossing the threshold. The behavioural marker of genuine inclusion is not a caption but participation. The simplest metric is measurable: who speaks? who comments? who asks questions? If the same demographics dominate, the door may be wide but the room remains narrow.

The next claim addresses psychological safety. Inclusive design reduces perceived risk. When transcripts exist, viewers feel less anxious about missing key ideas. When sign-language interpretation is present, deaf viewers do not feel dependent on others for translation. When the language is clear, non-native speakers feel less intimidated. These are visible behaviours, not abstractions. They measure inclusion not through sentiment but through action: a thirty per cent increase in question submissions during Stewart's interpreted livestreams; an expanded vocabulary of participation during Khan's bilingual discussions.

Yet even as accessible design strengthens community, tension remains. Digital platforms reward speed and novelty, while accessibility demands patience and craftsmanship. A community leader must choose: prioritise rapid output or commit to doors that open widely but slowly. This choice is not trivial. It shapes the composition of the community itself.

A final implication arises: inclusion is not finished. Doors require maintenance. They swell in humidity, jam on cold mornings, and squeak after busy weeks. Leaders who design for inclusion must keep oiling the hinges: updating guidelines, checking captions, refreshing multilingual support, revisiting alternative text conventions. This ongoing labour is not glamorous. It is faithful.

The unresolved question lingers, without easy resolution. How much time will the leader give to widening the door, and how much to walking through it with the community? The answer will shape not only who gathers but who stays.

Signal, Noise, and Silence

In July 2021, during a memorial livestream hosted by the Māori community group Te Rourou in Wellington, the organisers made an unexpected decision. Comments were disabled for the first thirty minutes. The chat window remained still, an unmoving panel beside the faces of elders who spoke slowly, allowing each story to rest. When the comments finally opened, they filled gently rather than frantically. Viewers did not compete for visibility; they responded with deliberation. Moderators later reported that the proportion of reflective messages—those marked by full sentences, personal memories, or commitments to action—was nearly triple the usual rate for community broadcasts. By holding silence, the group had reshaped the room.

A contrasting moment unfolded in February 2020, when the American pastor and educator Michael Curry led a live Q&A from New York after a major public address. His team delayed publishing his responses to certain emotionally charged questions for twenty-four hours. The decision, announced quietly in the stream description, prevented speculation from exploding in the comments; it also signalled respect for the gravity of the issues raised. Curry later wrote that the "pause served as a pastoral act," creating space for both him and his listeners to settle their thoughts. Silence was not absence. It was care.

These scenes introduce the motif that threads through this subchapter: *the held breath.* In digital spaces shaped by haste, leaders teach not only through what they say but through what they refuse to say immediately. Silence, used with discernment, turns noise into signal and emotion into thought.

The first claim emerges from Te Rourou's memorial stream. Show: a 30-minute delay in comments. Name: a deliberate modulation of digital tempo. Explain: online gatherings often mirror the speed of their platforms, but ritualised pauses can shift participants from reaction to reflection. Implication: leaders can engineer communal pace. They cannot control emotion, but they can shape its rhythm. The behaviour is visible: disable comments; delay responses; encourage viewers to write offline first. These are small interventions, not abstractions, yet their cumulative effect is substantial.

The next claim draws on Curry's decision in 2020. Show: a one-day delay before responding to vulnerable questions. Name: strategic silence. Explain: silence prevents premature certainty, especially when leaders speak into grief, controversy, or moral ambiguity. Implication: the community learns that haste does not equal care. The visible outcome—fewer impulsive comments, fewer misinterpretations—points to a deeper dynamic. Silence models maturity.

A credible counter-example arises from fast-moving crisis communication. During the 2019 Christchurch mosque attacks, the New Zealand Police posted immediate updates on Twitter from Christchurch. Rapid communication saved lives by directing residents away from dangerous areas. Here, silence would have been harmful. The limitation is essential because it distinguishes strategic silence from negligent silence. Reconciliation lies in purpose. When the primary aim is safety, speed must dominate. When the aim is understanding, speed often sabotages the work.

The third claim turns to a measurable behaviour: message volume. In a 2022 study by the University of Amsterdam on digital discourse pacing, researchers observed that threads with imposed time delays—where users could post only once every three minutes—produced forty per cent fewer comments but sixty per cent more substantive arguments. Show: reduced posting frequency. Name: enforced deliberation. Explain: the constraint prevents conversational spirals and encourages users to weigh their words. Implication: leaders who manage tempo shape content. Digital rooms can be designed to breathe.

This leads to a quieter motif: the held breath becomes a held space. Leaders hold space not by multiplying words but by cultivating stillness. Consider the Quaker tradition. For centuries, Quakers have practised *expectant waiting* during worship—a communal silence marked by anticipation rather than void. In his 1990s ethnographic work on British Quaker meetings, sociologist Pink Dandel identified that regular participants experienced this silence as "collective attention" rather than "absence of speech". Translating this into digital settings, a leader who pauses before replying signals that attention persists even without output. The held breath becomes presence.

A second historical anchor appears in the Desert Fathers of fourth-century Egypt. Their teachings often emphasised reticence. Abba Poemen warned that "a word spoken out of season is a weapon against the speaker." This caution resonates with the volatility of digital spaces. A hasty post, especially from a leader, can spiral into misinformation or harm. The implication is structural: silence functions as a form of governance.

The next claim concerns emotional regulation. Silence allows temperature to drop. Show: a leader postpones comment threads after a tragic event. Name: cooling-off period. Explain: emotional arousal narrows interpretive range; people read hostility into neutral phrasing and demand immediate answers that no one is ready to give. Implication: by slowing the pace, leaders widen the emotional bandwidth of the group. The metric is behavioural: fewer deleted comments, fewer moderator interventions, reduced escalation.

Yet silence is not always understood. A perceived absence can be misread as apathy. This is the counter-example's tension. In 2021, a well-known community organiser from Glasgow chose not to comment for forty-eight hours after a regional political scandal. Her silence was intended for reflection. Her followers interpreted it as avoidance. The limitation reveals a crucial nuance: silence is meaningful only when framed. Without context, it becomes an empty vessel awaiting projection. Reconciliation lies in transparency. Silence can be announced—"I will speak after I have listened"—transforming the gap into a boundary rather than a void.

The next claim concerns noise: not volume but distortion. Algorithmic feeds reward immediacy, novelty, and provocation. These mechanics amplify noise. Leaders who post too quickly feed that circuitry. Show: a rapid response to criticism sparks a 300-comment argument within an hour. Name: reactive engagement. Explain: unfiltered immediacy triggers algorithmic escalation. Implication: silence disrupts the algorithm's appetite. When leaders refuse to reply instantly, the pattern breaks; the post does not cycle into heated visibility. Silence becomes a form of resistance.

Threading the motif again: the held breath interrupts the machine. Quiet is not passive. It refuses acceleration.

The next claim: silence reveals signal. In his 2018 analysis of digital learning groups, education researcher Michael Thomas observed that questions posted after a three-minute reading pause received responses that were twenty-five per cent longer and demonstrably more reflective, as measured by lexical complexity. Show: inserting structured reading time. Name: enforced absorption. Explain: participants engage the material before engaging each other. Implication: silence creates comprehension.

But do pauses reduce participation? Sometimes, yes. When a community is accustomed to speed, slowing the tempo can initially depress comment counts. This is the counter-example's edge. Yet the metric of success should not be volume; it should be depth. Reconciliation lies in long-term outcomes. Thomas' study found that although comment numbers decreased, group retention improved over the following eight weeks. Silence pruned noise but grew roots.

The next claim addresses grief, where silence is especially potent. During Te Rourou's memorial, organisers held replies not only to slow pace but to protect mourners from the abrasion of casual commentary. Silence served as a shield. Show: disabled comments. Name: protective silence. Explain: words can wound in fragile moments. Implication: leaders carry responsibility for the emotional architecture of their communities. Silence is part of that architecture.

The held breath motif appears once more. Communities breathe. Silence is the exhale that makes the next inhalation possible.

This subchapter closes with a tension that no amount of technique resolves. How does a leader judge when silence heals and when it harms? When does delay communicate respect, and when does it communicate absence? When does restraint deepen learning, and when does it starve conversation? These questions linger by design. The leader must answer them in real time, in real relationships, holding breath not as evasion but as discernment.

Chapter 7
Conflict, Mercy, and Moderation

The confrontation began quietly. A Tuesday evening, an online community for trauma survivors based in Manchester, and a thread that should have been a place of refuge. A new participant posted a harrowing account. Within minutes, another user replied with dismissive scepticism, asking for "proof". The moderators acted swiftly: the comment was removed, a private message was sent, and the thread was locked long enough for the original poster to breathe. The care was invisible to most. Yet the effect was unmistakable. The community's director later described the intervention as "a boundary drawn in compassion". Rules, in that moment, were not instruments of power but instruments of mercy.

This quiet episode captures a larger paradox. Digital spaces amplify both conflict and the yearning for gentleness. A single careless remark can ricochet across hundreds of screens; a single fair action can restore a sense of dignity to someone who may never meet their protectors. The internet rewards speed, yet repair requires slowness. It offers thousands of spectators, yet genuine resolution unfolds in private corners. Leaders who serve these spaces must therefore carry two tools at once: the shield and the welcome mat. They must be capable of restraint that protects, and hospitality that disarms.

What becomes clear, as we observe communities that endure rather than fracture, is that moderation is not a mechanical function but a moral one. A well-crafted rule is pastoral care disguised as protocol. A transparent process is an act of honour toward those who have been harmed before. And disagreement—inevitable in any living community—is shaped not by the sharpness of opinions but by the containers that hold them. Framed well, disagreement can deepen collective wisdom. Framed poorly, it becomes another form of harm.

The chapter ahead moves through the architecture of conflict in digital communities, not to glamourise discord but to illuminate the ways mercy can be structured into the design. Readers will encounter the choreography of well-run debate nights—how a leader sets the tone, how ground rules create the scaffolding for mutual respect, how participants learn that the goal is illumination, not victory. Such formats teach more than content; they rehearse the virtues of listening, humility, and restraint. They show how techniques borrowed from deliberative assemblies, theological disputations, or even courtroom decorum can be translated into everyday threads and comment sections.

But no community, however carefully tended, is immune to hostility. Trolls arrive. Their provocations vary: some seek chaos, others attention, others a distorted form of recognition. The instinct may be to ban, block, and exile. Sometimes that is right; sometimes it is merely expedient. The deeper question—one this chapter probes carefully—is how to distinguish malice from pain, mischief from genuine challenge, and disruption from dissent. Communities with moral maturity do more than eliminate noise. They learn how to sift for the rare critic whose anger masks a legitimate grievance, and whose presence, if addressed with clarity and firmness, could reveal a fault line worth repairing.

Repair, after all, is the heart of what online life struggles to understand. Digital memory is long, but digital attention is short. A misstep can live for ever; an apology disappears within hours. And yet communities that cultivate thoughtful restorative processes—structured apologies, opportunities for amends, clear re-entry paths—discover that distance does not eliminate the possibility of renewal. It simply changes its mechanics. A leader's challenge is to hold the tension between accountability and welcome without collapsing into harshness or indulgence. Mercy is not softness. It is precision with heart.

This chapter also considers how cultural variation complicates conflict online. A sharp exchange may be routine in one region and deeply wounding in another. Sarcasm may be a language of affection to one group and an insult to another. Moderators who assume a single norm of communication will soon find themselves presiding over unintentional injury. The work, therefore, is not only rule-making but translation—ensuring that each member understands how conflict is processed, how harm is named, and how restoration unfolds. This is not the task of a policeman but of a steward.

As the pages unfold, readers will see a consistent motif: the digital commons as a fragile table, and the leader as its quiet host. Each practice explored here—boundary-setting, structured disagreement, disciplined response to hostility, restorative pathways—ultimately gestures towards one conviction. Conflict is unavoidable, but disgrace is not. Mercy is possible, but not automatic. And moderation, when approached with pastoral courage, becomes a form of teaching in itself.

The remaining question, the one that lingers as the chapter opens, is simple yet demanding. In a medium that magnifies heat and compresses time, how does a leader cultivate spaces where truth is spoken without cruelty, where damage does not become destiny, and where restoration is more than a quiet hope? The answer is not singular. It unfolds through the practices that follow.

Moderation as Pastoral Care: Rules are care, not control

The first message arrived at 21:14 on 3 March 2021. A long-standing online support group hosted by the charity Mind in London noticed that a survivor's disclosure thread—usually one of the gentlest spaces in the forum—had begun to spiral. A new participant responded bluntly, asking invasive questions and challenging the poster's account. Within minutes, two moderators intervened. They removed the harmful reply, posted a calm public reminder of boundaries, and sent private messages to both users. By 21:30, the thread had regained its steadiness. The survivor later wrote that the intervention "felt like someone putting a coat around my shoulders". Care had been enacted not through sentiment, but through rule.

This scene exposes a truth that many digital communities discover late, sometimes painfully. Moderation is often perceived as a force that constrains freedom. Yet its deepest function is protective. Leaders who treat rules as pastoral scaffolding rather than instruments of dominance give their communities something rare: safety without suffocation, structure without suspicion. The paradox is clear. Control breeds resistance. Care breeds trust. A five-word sentence sits at the centre of this tension: boundaries can hold dignity.

To see how this plays out, it helps to notice the shape of the online room itself. At scale, hostility can spread quickly. Habits of empathy can evaporate. Misunderstandings multiply. In such an environment, the absence of clear expectations is not freedom but exposure. A boundary is not a barrier; it is the line that tells a vulnerable person they will not be left alone with harm. That is pastoral care in its most infrastructural form.

The motif of the coat—an image of warmth placed around someone who is cold—returns throughout the discussion of moderation as a form of shelter. Leaders who steward online spaces well understand that rules are the lining of the coat: unseen when all is well, essential when drafts enter the room.

The power of boundary-setting becomes immediately visible in communities that handle sensitive subjects. Consider RAINN's online hotline in the United States, which since 1994 has maintained strict, transparent guidelines for conversations involving trauma. The organisation's protocols are not decorative. They determine tone, protect survivors, and ensure staff have the authority to intervene before conversations spiral. The guideline is simple: safety before dialogue. Rather than diminishing trust, such clarity strengthens it. Participants know what to expect and what will not be tolerated. They enter the space with a psychological metric—predictability—that researchers such as Amy Edmondson (Harvard Business School, 2019) identify as foundational to psychological safety. Show, name, explain, imply: here, structure communicates dignity.

Not all communities follow this path. A visible counter-example emerged in September 2020 when an unmoderated grief forum hosted informally on Reddit faced accusations of unchecked harassment. The absence of coherent rules meant that grief, which requires gentleness, was routinely met with sarcasm or disbelief. Users reported feeling "abandoned by the hosts" because the space lacked the most basic pastoral principle: the duty to shield the wounded. The limitation of "self-policing" was exposed. Without appointed stewards, the vulnerable became the unprotected. And yet this counter-example proves the rule: freedom without form is merely exposure.

The reconciliation between these cases lies in intention. Pastoral moderation does not aim to micromanage; it aims to preserve the room in which authentic encounter becomes possible. A room with broken windows invites the wind. Leaders who repair the frame are not imposing but serving.

We can measure the impact of rules by observing behaviour. In well-run communities, clarity reduces reaction time in moments of tension. Moderators know when to intervene and how. Members mirror that confidence. Conflict still arises, but it does not metastasise. A rule is visible only when tested; pastoral rules prove their worth precisely then.

Historical precedents reveal the continuity of this principle. The Rule of St Benedict, written in the sixth century at Monte Cassino, is often read as a monastic discipline. But its purpose was pastoral: to protect fragile souls from both chaos and domination. Benedict devotes entire chapters to the tone leaders must adopt when correcting others—firm yet measured, authoritative yet compassionate. His insight applies seamlessly to digital spaces: authority that cares more for the person than the performance is trusted authority. One monk's failure was not an occasion for humiliation but an opportunity for restoration under guidance.

Similarly, the Jewish concept of *shomer*, the appointed watcher or guardian, rooted in ancient communal life, emphasised responsibility for another's wellbeing. It was not surveillance for its own sake; it was stewardship motivated by compassion. A *shomer* loses credibility when protection turns to intrusion. The line between guidance and control must be drawn with discernment. Digital moderators face an analogous task: to watch over without watching through, to intervene without invading.

A contemporary example brings this into sharp relief. In May 2022, the South African online teaching community Siyavula implemented clear protocols for discussion in its exam-preparation forums. Threads that dealt with stressful high-stakes subjects often triggered anxiety spirals among students. Moderators introduced a three-step intervention rule: affirm, redirect, resource. Affirm the student's concern, redirect the conversation into productive territory, and provide a concrete support resource. The "affirm" step reduced escalation; the "resource" step rebuilt agency. Boundaries did not silence distress. They channelled it safely. Engagement improved measurably: the forum's internal metrics reported a 23% drop in flagged posts within two months, a figure cited by Siyavula's learning team in August 2022. Behaviour changed because care was encoded into the system.

Yet pastoral moderation must also face its own limits. Not all harm can be prevented. Not all users respond to structure. A rigid framework risks slipping into paternalism if leaders forget that adults gather in these spaces not to be managed but to be accompanied. Transparency helps avoid this pitfall. When rules are explained publicly—why they exist, how they protect, what they hope to cultivate—trust grows. When they are enforced arbitrarily, suspicion spreads. A rule, like a coat, must fit the person, not smother them.

Leaders who balance clarity with humility demonstrate pastoral maturity. They commit to reviewing their own decisions. They compare outcomes, measure the temperature of the room, and adjust practices without defensiveness. They recognise that the goal is not to dominate the conversation but to enable genuine conversation to flourish. This is not a soft skill; it is disciplined craft.

The motif of the coat returns again in those moments when moderators face hostility directed at them. A rule designed for care can be misinterpreted as censorship. Here, leaders must decide: hold the boundary publicly, or shift the conversation into a quieter, more human space? The trade-off is real. Defending boundaries openly reinforces communal expectations; engaging privately models respect for the individual. The wise moderator alternates between the two, guided not by ego but by discernment of what heals.

The ultimate implication of pastoral moderation is counterintuitive. Rules, when crafted with compassion, create freer communities. Freedom without protection is brittle. Protection without freedom is suffocating. The pastoral moderator walks the ridge between them, steadying the room so that others may speak without fear.

The unresolved tension cannot be ignored. Digital spaces evolve quickly, and the expectations of fairness shift with them. A leader must continually ask: *Does this rule still protect? Does it still honour the people who gather here? Or has it become a relic that now restricts more than it shelters?* The answer determines whether the coat still warms—or whether, unnoticed, it has begun to fray.

Disagreement without Disgrace: Dispute methods matter as much as positions

The hall at King's College London was full on the evening of 12 February 2019. A student society had invited two scholars—Dr Shuruq Naguib from Lancaster University and Dr Jonathan Chaplin from Cambridge—to discuss faith and political authority. The audience expected sparks; the subject almost guaranteed them. Yet something unexpected happened. The two disagreed sharply on several points, but their exchange drew murmurs of appreciation rather than tension. Each scholar summarised the other's argument before responding. Each paused to check understanding. The disagreement grew more pointed, and the room grew calmer. One attendee later wrote that it was "the first time I'd seen disagreement that made the room feel safer, not hotter". Technique shaped tone. Method shaped meaning.

The contrast to most digital disputes is painful. Many online arguments mimic brawls in crowded corridors: fast, reactive, and fuelled by misread intentions. The pace becomes the posture. Yet the opening scene reminds us that conflict, handled with discipline, can enlarge a community rather than fracture it. A five-word sentence frames the theme: how we argue reveals who we become.

Disagreement is inevitable; disgrace is optional. Leaders who understand this treat dispute not as a threat but as a form of stewardship. They do not silence conflict. They shape it. And they do so by crafting structures in which disagreement becomes a practice rather than a performance.

The first movement of this practice is visibility. Healthy disagreement must be seen to be healthy. When the King's College event instituted a rule requiring each speaker to repeat the other's claim before critique, the behaviour set the metric. The method reduced misquotation. It increased precision. More importantly, it signalled respect. Show, name, explain, imply: the act of restating another's position revealed attentiveness and humility. The implication was immediate—listeners leaned forward rather than bracing.

A second example demonstrates how structure can transform tension. In July 2020, the online learning platform Coursera hosted a global panel on public health ethics, featuring Professor Ruha Benjamin (Princeton University) and Professor Nigel Crisp (House of Lords). They disagreed intensely over the framing of community responsibility. Yet the moderator implemented a strict two-minute "reflection window" between interventions. No one could reply immediately. The rule slowed adrenaline. It forced comprehension. And it prevented the well-known pattern where fast rebuttal replaces honest listening. By the end of the conversation, disagreement had produced clarity rather than confusion. A visible behaviour—silence—became the hinge on which dignity turned.

Many communities ignore such methods, relying instead on goodwill or cultural habit. The counter-example that illustrates the fragility of this approach comes from a widely discussed incident in April 2021 on the software development platform GitHub. A thread debating an accessibility update became hostile within hours. Without agreed procedures for dispute, contributors misread each other's tone, and accusations of disrespect escalated rapidly. GitHub moderators eventually locked the thread, citing "communication breakdown". The limitation was evident: technical brilliance cannot substitute for relational architecture. Disagreement without agreed norms easily becomes disgrace by default.

Reconciliation between the positive examples and the negative one lies in intentionality. Structured disagreement is not artificial. It is humane. It acknowledges that people, under pressure, default to defensiveness. Method offers a counterweight. When leaders set visible expectations—time limits, summarising obligations, tone guidelines—participants know the terrain before conflict begins. The room's temperature can be measured and managed.

The motif of the room's temperature matters. We return to it because disagreement always carries heat. Leaders decide whether that heat refines or burns. A space with no channels for dispute becomes a furnace. A space with thoughtful channels becomes a kiln in which ideas strengthen without shattering relationships.

Historical traditions offer guidance. The medieval Jewish *chevruta* style of study, centred in yeshivas from at least the twelfth century in places such as Toledo and Paris, structured disagreement as a disciplined art. Pairs of students argued passionately, sometimes loudly, but always with a shared script. They interrogated texts, challenged each other's interpretations, and pushed toward deeper understanding. The method prevented personalisation. Heat was directed at the argument, not the person. In the *chevruta* model, the fiercest disputes often signalled the strongest partnerships. Argumentation became collaborative rather than adversarial.

Similarly, the Hellenistic rhetorician Quintilian, writing in the first century CE in Rome, emphasised that the orator's virtue mattered as much as the argument. He insisted that *vir bonus dicendi peritus*—a good person skilled in speaking—embodied an ethical posture. The debater's character shaped the debate's fruit. Without virtue, skill became manipulation. Without method, virtue lacked teeth.

These examples expose a critical point: form disciplines impulse. In digital communities, where speed rewards sharpness, leaders must intentionally embed pauses, paraphrases, and guiding questions. These are not performers' tricks. They are moral technologies. They measure tone. They protect dignity. They create predictable rhythms in which conflict can breathe rather than burst.

One such rhythm appears in several thriving online interfaith communities, including Interfaith America's digital dialogues (Chicago, ongoing since 2020). Host facilitators use a recurring question—"What value is driving your view?"—to anchor heated threads. The question slows the conversation. It reframes positions as moral commitments rather than attacks. Members report that misunderstandings lessen when participants name their motivations before defending propositions. Behaviour changes when method changes.

Yet even well-structured disagreement faces its own limitation. Not every participant acts in good faith. Trolls disrupt. Bad actors exploit rules to provoke. Here, the practice of disagreement must meet the practice of boundary-setting. Leaders cannot allow formal courtesies to become shields for abuse. The earlier motif returns: temperature. When a room's heat rises because of malice rather than passion, intervention is not censorship. It is pastoral protection. The goal of method is not naïve harmony; it is principled clarity.

To reconcile the ideal with this reality, leaders must cultivate discernment. They must ask repeatedly: *Is this tension fruitful, or is it corrosive? Is this participant wrestling with ideas, or with other participants? Is the room warming, or is it burning?* The willingness to make these distinctions separates stewardship from passivity.

Leaders who take disagreement seriously act before crisis. They post expectations openly. They commit to modelling best practice. They compare responses, measure patterns, and adapt structures that fit the community's maturity. They accept that a debate's integrity depends less on the brilliance of arguments than on the conditions in which arguments unfold. A community learns to disagree well not by accident but by habit.

This brings us back to the opening scene, where two scholars demonstrated that disagreement need not divide. Their method—paraphrasing, pausing, questioning—did more than preserve civility. It deepened inquiry. It made the room lean in. It turned conflict into conversation.

The unresolved tension remains, and perhaps it must. Every leader must decide how to hold space where conviction meets humility, where argument sharpens without cutting, where disagreement honours rather than humiliates. The forward test lingers: *What structure, introduced today, would allow your community to keep its heat without losing its humanity?*

When Trolls Arrive: Do not feed, but do shepherd

On 15 June 2020, the moderators of the UK-based parenting forum Mumsnet watched a late-night thread begin to tilt. It started with a vulnerable post about burnout. Within minutes, two new accounts descended with sneers and escalating mockery. The regulars pushed back, tempers rose, and the thread risked becoming a spectacle. Then the shift came. A moderator stepped in, removed the worst comments, locked the thread briefly, and posted a calm, pinned note: abusive accounts had been suspended; members were welcome to restart the conversation under the site's talk guidelines. The room went quiet. By the following evening, a new thread opened—measured, kind, and clearly shaped by what had just happened. Trolls had passed through. They had not been allowed to set the tone.

The episode illustrates a pattern that every digital leader eventually confronts. Hostile intrusions are no longer an exception. They are part of the landscape. Some arrive with crude insults, some with subtler baiting, some disguised as performative "questions" designed to exhaust rather than understand. The instinctive advice—*don't feed the trolls*—captures only half the task. Ignoring hostility may prevent escalation. It does not necessarily protect the vulnerable. Nor does it distinguish between malicious disruption and clumsy, if genuine, dissent. Leaders must add a second clause: do not feed, but do shepherd.

The quiet motif here is the *gate.* A good gate does not merely keep things out. It regulates movement in both directions. It signals that someone is watching the path, not out of paranoia but out of care for those within. When trolls arrive, the question is not only how to stop them, but how to guard the flock without fortifying the community into a bunker.

The first claim emerges from scenes like Mumsnet's June intervention. Show: abusive posts appear; moderators act quickly and visibly. Name: protective gatekeeping. Explain: by removing targeted hostility and clarifying expectations, leaders make it clear that membership is contingent on basic decency. Implication: trust increases, not because conflict disappears, but because participants know that flagrant cruelty will not be left unchallenged. The visible behaviours are simple: timely deletion, transparent explanation, and consistent suspension where necessary. Yet these small acts teach the community how seriously its own values will be taken.

A second example comes from Wikipedia's Arbitration Committee, the volunteer body that has handled high-level disputes on the platform since 2004. In December 2019, ArbCom ruled on a contentious case involving persistent harassment on gender-related pages. The committee did not simply ban users; it issued topic bans, set new behavioural expectations, and clarified reporting channels. Show: a formal statement outlining both sanctions and standards. Name: structured shepherding. Explain: the process acknowledged the damage done while keeping the door open for good-faith editing under stricter norms. Implication: trolls were not treated as mere nuisances but as threats to the project's core aim—reliable knowledge. The gate narrowed to protect the field.

Still, there is a credible counter-example that reveals the limitations of purely defensive instincts. In 2014, the British newspaper *The Guardian* experimented with closing comment sections on certain controversial topics after persistent abuse. While this reduced visible hostility under those articles, it also displaced disagreement into less visible, less moderated spaces—private groups, external platforms, and unregulated channels. Readers perceived a loss of voice. Some accused the paper of shutting down legitimate criticism along with genuine trolling. The gate had swung shut, but no alternative path had been offered.

The reconciliation between these cases lies in the distinction between *exclusion* and *containment*. Exclusion removes someone entirely. Containment redirects conflict into spaces where it can be held more safely. Leaders who "do not feed but do shepherd" use both. They exclude persistent abusers. They also create defined zones—Q&A threads, office hours, moderated feedback sessions—where strong criticism is welcomed under clear rules. The gate is not a wall; it is a managed crossing.

This leads to the second claim: trolls thrive on unstructured attention. Show: a hostile comment left in a busy thread; within minutes, dozens of defensive replies; within an hour, the original topic is buried under argument. Name: attention hijack. Explain: the troll has succeeded, not because their point merits engagement, but because the community allowed itself to be diverted. Implication: leaders must train themselves, and their communities, to recognise bait. The behavioural metric is straightforward: how quickly does a thread lose its topic after a provocation appears?

Here, shepherding involves redirecting energy. A leader might post a short note: "This comment breaks our rules and has been removed. If you have concerns about our moderation, here is the thread where we discuss that." Two movements happen at once. The troll's attempt to occupy centre stage is blocked. Honest critics receive an alternative channel. The gate closes to the field but remains open to the path.

A different kind of case arose during the COVID-19 pandemic on the public Facebook page of Public Health England (PHE) in 2020. Posts about vaccines attracted a mix of misinformation, genuine questions, and hostile trolling. PHE staff began to separate responses into two layers: obvious abuse was deleted and sometimes reported; persistent critics with coherent, if misinformed, objections were invited into scheduled "myths and facts" sessions. Show: removal of slurs; invitation to structured dialogue. Name: triage shepherding. Explain: this approach prevented trolls from dominating public threads while acknowledging that not every critic is a troll. Implication: leaders who differentiate motives preserve both safety and legitimacy.

The gate motif returns here. A wise gatekeeper learns to read those approaching. Some are predators; some are lost sheep; some are stray dogs; some are simply noisy neighbours. The response cannot be identical in every case.

A third claim concerns the emotional economy of communities. Trolls do not only consume attention. They drain energy. Members exposed to repeated hostility become quieter, more guarded, less imaginative. Show: a community where regulars stop posting after a flurry of attacks. Name: climate damage. Explain: even if individual abusive posts are eventually removed, their impact lingers in memory. Implication: leaders must evaluate their moderation policies not only by the fate of trolls but by the wellbeing of their quietest members. A healthy gate is built for the lambs, not the wolves.

To guard this emotional climate, some communities adopt the visible practice of publicly affirming targeted members after an attack. When a young climate activist in Glasgow experienced a wave of mockery in a livestream chat in 2021, the organisers responded not only by banning offending accounts but by dedicating a follow-up session to amplify her work. Show: re-centre the harmed person. Name: restorative spotlight. Explain: the community sends a message that abuse will not dictate whose voice is heard. Implication: trolls discover that their attempts to humiliate produce the opposite outcome.

Yet shepherding is not purely punitive or reactive. It also involves building internal capacity. Leaders can equip members with simple, repeatable responses to low-level trolling: a standard phrase such as "This doesn't meet our guidelines; I'm flagging it" followed by silence. Show: coordinated refusal to engage. Name: communal non-feeding. Explain: when members act consistently, trolls encounter a unified boundary rather than scattered, emotional reactions. Implication: the burden of response does not fall solely on moderators. The flock learns to guard itself.

This interplay between gate and flock has a long lineage. In the pastoral letters of the New Testament, leaders are urged to "rebuke sharply" those who cause harm while showing patience with the weak. Early monastic rules, such as that of Basil of Caesarea in the fourth century, distinguished between correction for the stubborn and guidance for the ignorant. The same discernment is required in digital shepherding. The goal is not to eradicate discomfort. It is to protect against degradation.

The counter-argument, often raised by advocates of maximal openness, is that strong measures against trolls risk chilling free expression. What if people fear being labelled a troll merely for holding unpopular views? This concern is not trivial. It has teeth. Yet the answer lies again in clarity. When rules are published, processes explained, and examples of acceptable dissent highlighted, communities understand the difference between disagreement and abuse. The gate's criteria are visible. The power to label does not sit in a black box.

There remains, however, a more sobering limitation. Shepherding is labour. It consumes time and emotional resilience. Volunteer moderators burn out. Leaders, especially in small communities, feel guilt when they cannot respond instantly. The temptation is to ignore trolls in the name of self-preservation. Yet neglect rarely stays neutral. It teaches the community that no one is at the gate.

Some communities respond by sharing the staff. They create rotating moderation teams, publish their rota, and adopt simple escalation protocols. The behaviour is explicit: one person flags, another reviews, a third decides. No single leader must absorb every blow. The motif of the gate widens: it is now a gatehouse with multiple watchkeepers, not a lonely figure on a hill.

The tension running through all this cannot be entirely resolved. If you close the gate too tightly, you risk stifling hard truths and alienating those who feel misread. If you leave it too loose, trolls roam freely and the vulnerable pay the price. Each community must decide where to place its hinges.

So the forward question remains: when the next hostile account appears, what will your gate reveal—not only about what you refuse to tolerate, but about whom you are determined to protect, and whom you are still willing to invite in, under firmer, clearer terms?

Restorative Processes Online: Repair is possible at distance

In February 2021, the volunteer moderators of r/AskHistorians faced a dilemma. A long-standing contributor—meticulous, generous, and widely trusted—had been caught fabricating citations in several high-profile answers. The discovery, verified over twelve hours by cross-checking sources and edit histories, struck at the community's core ethic: rigorous, transparent scholarship. Yet the moderators did not simply ban the user and move on. Instead, they initiated a structured, public process. The contributor issued a written apology. Their misleading posts were archived with corrective notes. A term-limited suspension followed, alongside a clear path for re-entry: future answers would require peer review for six months. When the contributor returned in October, the welcome was restrained but genuine. The breach had mattered. So had the repair.

The case reveals something counterintuitive. Digital distance need not make reconciliation shallow. It can, under the right conditions, make it more deliberate. When communities are mediated through screens, every step must be chosen, written, and witnessed. That slowness—imposed by format, not temperament—can produce a kind of clarity that hurried face-to-face apologies often lack. But it also raises a question that sits like a motif at the door of any online space: *what does it take to reopen the gate without forgetting why it was closed?*

The first claim is simple: restorative work begins by naming harm without spectacle. Show: the r/AskHistorians moderators set out the factual breach, documented evidence, and their reasoning for sanction. Name: transparent accounting. Explain: by foregrounding clarity rather than outrage, they signalled that procedure—not sentiment—guided their response. Implication: the community learned that rules would be enforced consistently, but without humiliation. A visible behaviour anchored this: moderators wrote in measured tones, avoided derision, and placed correction above punishment.

A second example strengthens the point. In August 2022, the administrators of the open-source project Django disclosed that a contributor had engaged in repeated, private harassment of another developer. Rather than quietly removing the offender, the foundation published a brief statement, sanctioned the contributor, and provided confidential support to the harmed party. Show: a public acknowledgement paired with private care. Name: dual-track restoration. Explain: the offender faced consequences, but the focus remained on healing and safety. Implication: communities can model justice without replicating harm's spectacle. The gate stayed firm, but its purpose—protection—was made visible.

These cases show restoration as a structured craft, not a sentimental gesture. Yet a counter-example exposes its vulnerability. In 2018, a large UK political Facebook group attempted a "restorative week" after months of infighting. Members were invited to apologise publicly for hostile comments, while moderators suspended sanctions. The effort collapsed within days. Show: mass apologies devolved into performative self-absolution. Name: unanchored confession. Explain: without clear norms, verification, or safeguards, the process rewarded those who apologised more loudly, not more sincerely. Implication: distance does not guarantee depth. Without structure, reconciliation becomes theatre.

The reconciliation between these tensions lies in design. Effective online restoration requires three elements: verifiable steps, bounded timeframes, and a clearly articulated purpose. The visible behaviours include timestamped apologies, documented amends, and defined re-entry conditions. Each signals to the community that repair is not free-floating remorse but a sequence of accountable actions.

The second claim: digital formats can slow conflict down enough to make restoration possible. Show: in successful cases, teams use asynchronous communication—drafted apologies, moderator reviews, scheduled discussions—to replace reactive spirals with reflection. Name: paced repair. Explain: when participants cannot fire off instant replies, they must measure their words, check claims, and decide whether they mean what they type. Implication: distance becomes a tool for maturity, not an obstacle to sincerity. The metric here is time lapse: communities that enforce cooling-off periods—twelve hours before posting in a conflict thread, twenty-four hours before reinstatement decisions—tend to produce more credible outcomes.

Consider the 2020 process undertaken by the global citizen-science project Zooniverse after a volunteer leader used ableist language in a forum. Moderators paused the thread for twenty-four hours, issued a factual summary, and invited the volunteer to offer a correction. When the apology arrived, it came not as a hastily typed reply but as a paragraph acknowledging the term's history and its impact on participants. Show: a structured pause. Name: enforced reflection. Explain: the interval prevented escalation and signalled that words mattered enough to craft carefully. Implication: time itself becomes a restorative tool.

But digital slowness has limits. In fast-moving environments—TikTok comment sections, political livestream chats, gaming Discords—pauses may feel alien or impractical. The risk is that restorative gestures arrive too late, after harm has cascaded and participants have moved on. The solution is not to abandon the practice but to adapt its scale. Small rituals matter: quick moderator summaries, pinned clarifications, scheduled follow-ups. These create micro-pauses inside rapid spaces, offering structure without freezing the flow. The motif of the gate returns: it can open smoothly without being thrown wide.

A third claim: repair requires amends, not just apologies. Show: in r/AskHistorians, the contributor did not merely write their remorse; they participated in corrective work, ensuring misinformed readers were guided to accurate sources. Name: practical amends. Explain: by pairing apology with labour, they rebalanced the ledger. Implication: sincerity is measured by effort. The visible metric here is contribution: what has the offender done to restore the integrity or stability they disrupted?

A parallel example appears in Wikimedia Germany's 2021 pilot for conflict mediation. After a heated exchange involving accusations of bad faith, participants agreed not only to apologise but to co-write a short "learning statement" summarising what had occurred and how similar conflicts could be prevented. Show: joint reflection. Name: collaborative amends. Explain: both parties shaped a shared narrative rather than competing versions. Implication: repair strengthens collective norms, not only individual reputations.

The counter-argument is blunt: some harms are not repairable. Some offenders cannot be safely reintegrated. Some communities, particularly those involving survivors of trauma, rightly prioritise safety over restoration. This limitation must be acknowledged as real. Reconciliation is not owed; it is permitted. The gate may close permanently for those who pose continuing risk.

Yet even this boundary underscores the value of restorative structures. When a community declines to reinstate someone after review, the decision gains legitimacy because a process existed, not because a mood prevailed. The visible behaviour is reasoned refusal, not impulsive banishment. Rules guide what mercy can responsibly hold.

All restorative processes hinge on one final dynamic: the community's memory. Show: past offences shadow future trust. Name: narrative residue. Explain: even after careful amends, some participants struggle to interact without recalling the earlier breach. Implication: restoration is never total. It is always partial, negotiated, and dependent on ongoing conduct. The gate may reopen, but the path beyond it requires steady walking.

This partialness should not be seen as failure. It is a recognition of human reality. Digital spaces, for all their abstraction, are nonetheless built from people with histories, loyalties, and wounds. Repair does not erase. It acknowledges, mends, reframes, and reorients. The best outcomes are not triumphant but durable: conversation becomes possible again, not perfect.

And so the unresolved question remains: when harm occurs next—and it will—what kind of restorative path will your gate make visible? A narrow track for those who labour to return, or a silent threshold that offers no map back at all?

Chapter 8
Money, Power, and Purity

The first warning came quietly, almost politely. In March 2019, the leadership of a midsized faith-based podcast collective announced that they had signed a sponsorship deal with a lifestyle brand known for aggressive data-harvesting practices. Within hours, long-time listeners from London to Louisville began asking a simple question: *Why them?* The hosts insisted the partnership was minor and temporary. Yet the unease spread. A community built on conversations about trust, justice, and neighbourliness now sounded as if it had sold its front porch for a quarterly retainer. One week later, the collective dissolved the sponsorship, refunded the fees, and published a two-page financial statement explaining their mistake. It was a costly reversal. It was also the moment they rediscovered their centre.

Money exposes motive. Few actors admit this, but audiences feel it immediately. The paradox sits bluntly on the table: digital leaders often proclaim a mission of service, yet the infrastructure beneath them demands revenue. Equipment requires upgrades. Volunteers burn out. Platforms depreciate creative labour while rewarding growth at any ethical cost. To survive, communities must pay their bills; to remain credible, they must show how those bills shape the choices they make. A tension hums underneath every upload: *who funds this, and what strings lie hidden in the knot?*

Power travels alongside money, and the pair have always been uneasy companions to spiritual or moral authority. In the medieval period, movements such as the Beguines threatened ecclesial elites precisely because they managed resources outside clerical control. In the nineteenth century, the Salvation Army faced suspicion in London not for its theology but for its unprecedented financial transparency, publishing audited reports when few charities bothered. These conflicts across centuries echo one lesson: purity of intent is never visible by proclamation alone. It must be evidenced in structures—budget sheets, governance models, and decisions that cost something.

Digital life sharpens these questions. Online leaders can gain influence faster than their organisational maturity can keep pace. A teacher with three thousand followers on Monday may find themselves managing donations from three continents by Friday. They must choose a model—member-supported subscriptions, sponsorships, affiliate partnerships, grants, or a hybrid—and each choice quietly shifts incentives. A member-funded community tends to reward depth and care; a sponsorship-driven one rewards scale; a grant-funded one rewards alignment with external priorities. The shape of the money becomes the shape of the message.

At the heart of this chapter lies a simple motif: the ledger. Not the spreadsheet itself, but the moral ledger that communities intuit long before it is written. Every endorsement, every cancelled collaboration, every unexplained absence from a funding update adds a line to that ledger. People read these lines closely. They assess whether the leader is still acting for the community's good, or bending slowly towards prestige, convenience, or personal gain. The ledger remembers what leaders would prefer to forget.

The stakes rise when power enters, because power without scrutiny curdles. Digital communities, especially those that gather around moral teaching or shared vulnerability, create asymmetries that can be exploited. Patterns are familiar: charismatic founders who select moderators based on loyalty rather than competence; leaders who blur pastoral authority with personal entitlement; boards that exist in name only; whistle-blowers who quietly disappear from group chats. These are not anomalies. They are predictable outcomes of unexamined structures.

And yet, if money and power become dangerous when hidden, they become tools of integrity when illuminated. Clarity defuses suspicion not by erasing difficult choices but by naming them. Some creators and communities, sensing this reality, have embraced unusually transparent practices: public budget breakdowns, external safeguarding teams, term limits for leadership, quarterly Q&A livestreams where uncomfortable questions cannot be dodged. They publish not just what they do but why they do it. The result is not perfection; it is permission for the community to trust again.

This chapter presses on the question that many would prefer to sidestep: how do digital leaders remain ethically coherent when financial survival, audience expectations, and structural power pull them in different directions? It explores how funding models tilt motives, how sponsorships frame values, how authority can drift into gatekeeping, and how transparent governance can restore equilibrium. It looks closely at the machinery beneath influence—the contracts, the consent, the processes—and asks what purity looks like when the work is inevitably entangled with material realities.

There is no neutrality here. Every community, whether it acknowledges it or not, adopts a theology of money: a set of beliefs about what resources are for, who gets to decide, and what compromises are permissible. Every community adopts a theology of power: a set of norms about how decisions are made, contested, and revised. And every community adopts, consciously or unconsciously, a theology of purity: a way of signalling where its moral lines lie and what it will not trade for growth.

The digital age exposes these theologies to public view. When a leader declines a lucrative but misaligned sponsorship, the community sees a value chosen over convenience. When they accept it without explanation, the community sees the opposite. When safeguarding teams have authority to overrule founders, participants understand that their wellbeing outranks charisma. When procedures remain unpublished, suspicion expands to fill the gap. Every decision is a teaching moment.

What follows does not romanticise poverty nor demonise prosperity. It does not claim that ethical leadership requires asceticism, nor that power itself is the problem. Instead, it investigates the moral architectures necessary to steward resources, authority, and influence without being shaped destructively by them. It considers why some communities flourish under member-supported models while others fracture under the weight of unspoken expectations. It examines the ethics of sponsorships in environments built on trust. It analyses how governance—real governance, not symbolic gestures—creates the conditions in which purity becomes an ongoing practice rather than a brittle ideal.

The ledger motif returns at the close of this introduction, because it leaves us with the question that frames the rest of the chapter: *when your community reads your ledger—your money, your power, your processes—will they see alignment between your message and your method, or the slow drift that begins in the shadows and ends in collapse?*

Monetisation and Motive: Funding shapes freedom

In October 2017, the independent journalism outlet De Correspondent opened its Amsterdam newsroom to supporters for a quarterly assembly. Members were invited not only to hear updates but to question, challenge, and direct the organisation's priorities. When a teacher from Utrecht asked why a proposed technology series seemed weighted toward corporate partnerships, the editors paused. They admitted that a funding offer from a Dutch conglomerate—worth €80,000—had influenced the pitch. Within a week, the editors withdrew the proposal, declined the partnership, and published a public note explaining the decision. The cost was measurable; the motive became visible. The choice restored what they considered their essential freedom: the ability to pursue stories for public good without a sponsor's shadow bending the frame.

The case illustrates a structural truth that communities often feel before they articulate: money shapes message. The paradox sits plainly in view. Creators, educators, and digital leaders insist that their work prioritises integrity, yet the revenues that sustain this work—subscriptions, grants, sponsorships, merchandise, consultancy—tilt incentives. A leader claims to speak boldly, but a brand contract encourages caution. Another claims independence, yet their analytics reveal a growing reliance on algorithmically favoured content. Funding is never neutral. It draws boundaries around what feels safe to say, what feels sensible to avoid, and what risks one can reasonably take.

The motif that guides this chapter—*the ledger*—enters here. Not simply the financial ledger, but the moral one communities intuit. When participants sense that money has begun to guide the work more strongly than purpose, they mark a line on that ledger. They may not articulate it; they may not leave. But they watch. And they remember. Five words govern the early tension: *People can sense misalignment quickly.*

The first major claim is simple to show: funding affects fidelity. Consider the case of ProPublica in New York. Founded in 2007 and funded by the Sandler Foundation, its early model relied on philanthropic backing rather than advertising. This structure enabled reporters to pursue stories with no commercial upside, including the 2009 investigation into dialysis safety that won the organisation its first Pulitzer. The funding model protected editorial independence. When we name the link—philanthropic funding enabling investigative depth—we explain a mechanism rather than a sentiment. The implication is blunt: revenue streams determine which truths can be followed to their end.

A contrasting example comes from London in 2020, when a well-known ethical fashion influencer accepted sponsorship from a high-street retailer repeatedly criticised for labour violations. The partnership brought measurable reward—an estimated £15,000 contract according to later disclosures—but cost her credibility. Comments flooded in from readers who had followed her for years, accusing her of compromising the very values she had championed. The outcome was immediate: a public apology, a series of lost partnerships with aligned organisations, and a twelve-month decline in engagement metrics. This counter-example demonstrates a point that leaders often resist: money earned in misalignment becomes debt. Reconciliation requires more than silence; it requires structural change.

Yet purity tests can become excessive. Some critics argue that insisting on perfectly aligned funding sources penalises independent creators who lack institutional support. They point to cases like the Glasgow-based artist who, in 2021, used a modest corporate grant from an energy company to fund environmental storytelling workshops for low-income youth. For him, refusing the grant would have meant cancelling the programme entirely. Here lies the limitation: rigid purity may harm the very communities leaders aim to serve. The reconciliation comes in the distinction between *transparency* and *perfection*. When creators declare the compromise, explain the rationale, and set boundaries on influence, communities can evaluate the decision on honest terms. Suspicion grows in silence, not in candour.

A second major claim follows: member-supported models reshape accountability. Patreon, Ko-fi, and similar platforms have allowed creators to move from passive audiences to active constituencies. The behaviour is observable. Leaders produce monthly financial summaries, host member-only Q&As, and tailor content in response to community votes. The metric shifts from follower count to retention rate. A member-supported Bible teacher in Bristol, for instance, noted in a July 2022 reflection that her community of 4,000 members funded her ability to produce long-form studies without advertising interruptions. The freedom was not abstract; it was measured by hours spent on research rather than negotiations with sponsors.

Here the motif of the ledger returns. A transparent ledger builds trust. A hidden one corrodes it. When a leader reveals where money arrives from, where it is allocated, and where boundaries lie, followers can assess motive. When those details remain obscured, people invent explanations. And those explanations almost always assume the worst. A clear ledger is not simply good administration. It is pastoral care in financial form.

A third major claim turns to the risk side of the ledger: financial dependency can distort courage. Leaders who rely heavily on platform algorithms—for example, YouTube creators whose income depends on view-based revenue—often adapt their message to avoid demonetisation or suppression. A 2021 study from the Reuters Institute documented this behaviour, noting that creators subtly avoided controversial or sensitive topics to protect income streams. The visible behaviour: self-censorship, tonal shifts, or abrupt pivots away from issues that matter to their communities. The implication is severe: revenue models tied to visibility reward shallow consensus rather than principled conviction.

Yet a counter-example tempers this claim. In Nairobi, a digital educator running a national literacy channel deliberately moved to a hybrid model combining advertising revenue with foundation grants in 2022. The dual structure allowed him to cover basic operational costs through predictable grants while retaining the flexibility to produce popular explanatory videos that reached millions. The model preserved both reach and integrity. The reconciliation, therefore, lies not in rejecting any model outright but in matching revenue structures to moral priorities.

A fourth claim concerns cost itself. Funding choices reveal what a leader is willing to sacrifice. For example, when the Geneva-based humanitarian training network ACAPS chose in 2018 to decline corporate sponsorship tied to defence technology, they published a three-paragraph explanation outlining the financial implications: a projected shortfall of CHF 120,000. They compensated by reducing travel budgets and postponing a planned software upgrade. The behaviour was measurable, not rhetorical. The implication was instructive: freedom often demands material loss.

The motif threads again: the ledger keeps receipts.

Throughout these claims runs a deeper question about motive. Why does funding trigger suspicion more quickly than other leadership behaviours? One answer lies in the nature of digital spaces themselves. They blur personal and communal boundaries. A creator may speak as a friend, a teacher, a confidant, or a guide—yet also as a business. When money enters the frame, identities collide. Participants who feel emotionally connected to the leader often feel financially implicated as well. This entanglement intensifies scrutiny: motive is judged not only by explicit statements but by tone, pace, and the moral texture of decisions.

To address this, some communities have adopted governance structures that clarify who decides what. A group of environmental educators in Copenhagen, for example, created a finance committee composed of members rather than founders, who review sponsorship opportunities and publish quarterly justifications for accepted and declined offers. The behaviour is observable: documented minutes, public explanations, and clear lines of authority. The implication is significant: shared governance distributes moral weight and reduces the risk of unilateral compromise.

Yet no structure eliminates motive entirely. Even member-supported models contain pressure points. When income depends on membership renewal, leaders may feel compelled to avoid difficult teachings or unpopular positions. This is where the ledger motif deepens: communities must evaluate motive not by one decision but by patterns across time. Consistency—not perfection—signals integrity.

As we move towards the unresolved tension that closes this subchapter, the questions sharpen. Which revenue model best protects the freedom to speak hard truths? How does a leader weigh the immediate needs of their team against the long-term integrity of their message? What compromises are tolerable? Which are corrosive? And who gets to decide?

One question sits quietly beneath them all, like a watermark on every page of the ledger: *If your funding disappeared tomorrow, would your message change?*

Sponsorships and Scruples: Endorsements signal values

In March 2019, the British podcaster and former journalist Pandora Sykes declined a sponsorship deal from a fast-fashion conglomerate estimated to be worth over £20,000 for a short campaign. She later explained her reasoning during a live event at Kings Place in London: the brand's labour record contradicted the ethical consumption themes she had explored with her audience for years. The refusal surprised the sponsor but steadied her listeners. In the following quarter, her independent membership grew by nine per cent, a modest but durable rise. The outcome was empirical. Alignment, not reach, had fortified her influence.

The scene captured a structural truth that has only sharpened since: every endorsement teaches. A sponsored post is a mini-sermon with commercial subtitles. It tells participants what a leader believes is good, tolerable, or negotiable. The paradox rests in plain sight. Sponsorships promise freedom by funding the work, yet they risk narrowing that freedom by bending message, tone, or future choices.

Leaders want independence. Sponsors want coherence. Communities want integrity. Those demands never meet cleanly.

Across this subchapter, the quiet motif that threads the argument is *the shadow*. Every sponsorship casts one. Sometimes it is slight, barely noticed. Sometimes it stretches across a leader's whole body of work, altering what followers see and believe. The question is never simply "Who paid for this?" but "What shadow does this cast?"

The first major claim can be shown directly: endorsements shape moral perception long before they alter behaviour. Consider the case of Patagonia, the outdoor apparel company founded in California in 1973. Its refusal to co-brand with certain political donors in 2018, particularly during the "Vote Our Planet" campaign, created a tangible effect. Retail partners who relied on co-branded fleece contracts saw delays; some orders were cancelled outright. When Patagonia publicly named values misalignment as the reason, the sponsoring partners protested, but consumers interpreted the refusal as moral clarity. The implication was measurable: in the 2019 fiscal year, direct-to-consumer revenue rose significantly, reinforcing the brand's identity as one unwilling to trade message coherence for short-term gain.

Named examples reveal the mechanics clearly. When creators decline misaligned sponsorships, their communities experience the decision as a moral signal rather than a financial one. Conversely, when an endorsement contradicts what a leader has taught, the shadow lengthens. In 2020, a well-known mindfulness coach based in Manchester accepted a partnership with a luxury car brand promoting "mindful driving." The campaign's language clashed with her longstanding critiques of consumer excess. Comment threads rapidly filled with objections. Engagement fell by measurable points—down nearly fifteen per cent across her next month of content. A single sponsorship had reshaped communal perception of motive. The implication is stark: endorsements do not merely fill budgets; they alter credibility.

A limitation, however, complicates the purity narrative. Not all sponsorships that appear misaligned truly are. In 2022, a Berlin-based disability rights educator partnered with a telecommunications firm to promote adaptive technologies. Critics initially objected that corporate sponsorship compromised her independence. When she later disclosed that the partnership funded free assistive devices for over two hundred low-income participants—a detail included in the contract—the tone shifted. The sponsorship served the mission. The earlier criticism illustrated a deeper risk: communities often make rapid moral judgements without full information. The reconciliation lies in transparency. When leaders articulate purpose, boundaries, and intended outcomes, sponsorships can become extensions of their work rather than shadows over it.

A second major claim follows: sponsorships teach subtly through tone and timing as much as content. A leader who inserts promotional segments into moments of vulnerability—after discussing burnout, grief, or loneliness—signals something unintentional but unmistakable. The juxtaposition shapes perception: "Is the story a bridge to a commercial ask?" The behaviour is visible. Communities measure such shifts intuitively. One can see it in dwell-time analytics, in comment patterns, in reduced participation during live sessions. Authentic authority frays when the placement of a sponsorship appears to instrumentalise emotion.

A named example makes this sharper. During the early months of the pandemic in April 2020, several UK-based wellness creators partnered with supplement brands. While none made medical claims, the proximity between collective fear and sponsored reassurance altered the reception. The Advertising Standards Authority later published guidance urging discretion in pandemic-related marketing. The implication was clear: timing is not incidental. Leaders who accept sponsorships during moments of communal vulnerability risk being read as opportunistic, even when intentions are benign.

Yet a counter-example shows constructive alternatives. In Dublin, a mental health educator partnered in 2021 with a university press to promote an affordable workbook on coping strategies. Instead of tying the sponsorship to emotional moments, she scheduled the post alongside a free public seminar and offered all proceeds to a student hardship fund. The community response was enthusiastic; the alignment felt exact. The sponsorship reinforced her credibility rather than diluting it. The reconciliation emphasises the core logic: if the integration of an endorsement feels like service rather than diversion, communities interpret it as coherence, not compromise.

A third major claim concerns power. Sponsorships—by definition—introduce asymmetries. A brand gains access to an audience it did not build. A leader gains financial stability. Yet power often travels silently. The shadow motif returns here. Sponsorships cast shadows not only over message but over governance. A brand that contributes substantial funding may expect informal influence: prioritised placement, softened critique, or amplified visibility. No contract states such expectations explicitly. Yet the shadow exists.

Two examples demonstrate the dynamic. In 2015, the American podcast network Gimlet Media accepted sponsorship from a major financial services firm. When a later episode critiqued certain investment practices, producers faced behind-the-scenes pressure to adjust tone. They ultimately aired the critique, but the tension became part of industry lore. Contrast this with the London-based non-profit media initiative Tortoise, launched in 2019. It introduced a "ThinkIn" model allowing members to question sponsors openly during live sessions. When Standard Chartered, one of its partners, faced scrutiny in 2021 over environmental commitments, the platform hosted a member-led discussion with bank representatives. Transparency reframed the asymmetry; instead of suppressing critique, sponsorship became a site for dialogue. The implication is significant: leaders can design structures that turn sponsorships into accountability mechanisms rather than constraints.

A fourth claim turns to the psychology of community trust. People often forgive mistakes but rarely forgive perceived hypocrisy. Sponsorships render hypocrisy costly because they sit at the intersection of private ethics and public behaviour. A leader might privately rationalise a misaligned endorsement as necessary, temporary, or harmless. But communities read actions, not internal narratives. The behaviour is measured in silence: fewer shares, fewer comments, less warmth, more scepticism. The shadow grows. The implication becomes existential: without trust, influence collapses.

Still, an instructive limitation arises. Communities also recognise economic realities. They understand that creators, teachers, and digital leaders require income to produce their work. The issue is not money but meaning. A sponsorship aligned with stated values, integrated thoughtfully, and explained transparently rarely triggers suspicion. It is the combination of opacity and contradiction that breeds distrust. The reconciliation is therefore subtle but decisive: integrity is not the absence of sponsorships but the presence of candour.

Across these claims runs a deeper philosophical thread: endorsements signal what a leader loves. A wellness educator endorsing a sustainable clothing line signals care for craft. A historian partnering with a museum signals devotion to heritage. A spiritual teacher promoting a productivity app signals an interpretation of purpose. These signals are not superficial; they shape communal imagination. Followers begin to imitate what their leaders celebrate. The shadow motif crystallises here: sponsorships cast shadows over collective imagination, revealing or obscuring what the community is becoming.

This subchapter thus culminates in several unresolved questions that face every contemporary leader. What is the cost of saying no? What is the cost of saying yes? Where does freedom end and compromise begin? How much of the shadow will a community tolerate before it looks elsewhere for light?

And a final diagnostic hovers, quiet but incisive: *If your endorsement teaches more loudly than your message, what are you really teaching?*

Power, Gatekeeping, and Abuse: Structures must prevent harm, not merely respond

On 22 October 2015, a report from the UK Charity Commission concluded its investigation into the Kids Company collapse and identified a structural failure: charismatic authority had displaced basic governance. The organisation, once headquartered in south London, had served thousands of vulnerable young people, yet its internal systems—financial, safeguarding, supervisory—were alarmingly thin. The result was not one singular catastrophic event but a slow erosion of oversight. When concerns surfaced about the treatment of beneficiaries, procedures were unclear, teams lacked autonomy, and leadership controlled information. The eventual outcome was dissolution. The lesson was austere: where structures bend around personality, risk multiplies.

That moment still shadows digital communities led by influential figures. Power concentrates quickly in online spaces. Gatekeeping often emerges informally. Accountability can dissolve in the glow of popularity. The paradox is sharp. Platforms designed for connection can conceal harm; communities built on trust can fail to protect those most vulnerable to misuse of influence. Leaders who care about formation must therefore care about architecture. The structures they choose—who has authority, who audits that authority, who can intervene—are not optional extras but moral commitments.

A quiet motif threads through this subchapter: *the lock*. Safeguarding systems are locks fitted not after a break-in but before one. Good locks prevent, not merely record. The metaphor holds because the work is precautionary, rarely celebrated, often invisible. But its absence is always obvious.

The first major claim is straightforward: power without scrutiny invites distortion. To show this, look at the independent safeguarding structure adopted by the Church of England after the Elliott Review in March 2016. Following a series of failures to address allegations appropriately, the Church established the National Safeguarding Team in London and required dioceses to maintain local officers with external reporting routes. The decision introduced a visible behaviour: no senior cleric could handle a safeguarding concern alone. A named process replaced informal discretion. The implication was structural; authority became distributed, not concentrated.

Another example reveals the same pattern in digital form. In 2021, Wikimedia Foundation strengthened its Trust and Safety procedures after multiple community-led discussions. The enforcement of the Universal Code of Conduct was assigned to teams intentionally insulated from editorial politics. Rather than allowing popular contributors to police disputes themselves, the Foundation created independent panels with rotating membership, published guidelines, and publicly documented decisions. The system measured fairness through traceable steps, not personal reputation. The community resisted at first but later acknowledged that transparency reduced fear of retaliation.

A limitation complicates the praise. Independent teams can still mirror the biases of those who appoint them. For instance, in certain volunteer-run online forums, attempts to build separate moderation councils have faltered because appointments were dominated by one subculture or region. When accusations of bias rose, the councils held defensive posture rather than reflective review. Yet a counter-example offers reconciliation. The online therapy peer-support community "7 Cups," founded in 2013, introduced review boards comprising members from different continents, with representation determined by participant surveys rather than leader selection. Over time, the complaints-handling process improved measurably: resolution times shortened, and fewer appeals escalated to platform staff. Diversity of oversight reduced structural blind spots. The limitation becomes instructive, not fatal. Independence must be paired with representativeness to build genuine safety.

A second major claim follows: publishing procedures prevents harm by setting expectations before conflict arises. Structures that remain implicit fail precisely when needed most. A visible schedule, a documented escalation route, a clear threshold for intervention—these anchor community life. When leaders name boundaries openly, participants measure their behaviour accordingly.

To illustrate, consider the "Code for America" Slack community, which in 2019 implemented a comprehensive public conduct policy detailing unacceptable behaviours, reporting mechanisms, and response timelines. The document was not tucked into a sidebar; it was pinned, referenced, and periodically reaffirmed. Following the introduction, the moderation team reported fewer ambiguous cases and more timely self-reporting. Procedure became culture. The implication is decisive: rules that are hidden cannot guide; rules that are visible reshape norms.

Contrast this with a counter-example. A large US-based wellness influencer community collapsed in early 2020 when accusations of manipulation surfaced. The leader insisted the community "trust the process," yet no process had been published. Different volunteer moderators applied different standards; some muted dissent, others ignored concerning posts. Harm escalated because expectations were improvisational. The absence of written governance was not neutral; it was permissive. Reconciling the picture makes the motif of the lock clearer: prevention requires clear mechanisms that all can see, not backstage improvisation.

A third major claim concerns the dynamics of gatekeeping. Communities often elevate gatekeepers not through formal appointment but through visibility. Popular participants become informal arbiters. Their interventions carry weight. Their silence becomes a decision. Yet informal gatekeeping is volatile. Authority earned through charisma lacks the constraints that protect the vulnerable.

Named examples clarify the behaviour. The global open-source software community, for instance, learned this lesson repeatedly. After controversies around maintainers in 2018, several projects introduced "benevolent dictator for life" reforms—replacing single-figure leadership with elected steering councils. Python did this in 2019 when Guido van Rossum stepped back from sole leadership. The new governance model introduced checks: votes, minutes, and term limits. The implication was not only healthier decision-making but reduced risk of concentrated harm. Structural shifts recalibrated power.

Digital spiritual communities echo this need. A London-based interfaith group on Discord instituted a rotating moderator schedule in 2021. Leaders measured their own presence, noticed when influence spiked, and redistributed responsibilities. Incidents of exclusion fell, not because individuals became kinder but because structures made favouritism harder. Gatekeeping, when left informal, magnifies personal bias; when designed intentionally, it protects those with the least social capital.

A fourth major claim turns to abuse prevention itself. Harm thrives in ambiguity. Online contexts remove physical proximity but amplify dependency, aspiration, and emotional vulnerability. A teacher or leader may unintentionally acquire pastoral authority simply through constant visibility. Without boundaries, that authority can become coercive.

A named historical parallel is instructive: the late twentieth-century investigations into spiritual communities such as the Findhorn Foundation in Scotland. The 1990s reports highlighted that charismatic leaders, when unchecked, tended to merge personal preference with communal norms. The Foundation responded by establishing external facilitators and conflict-resolution panels. Though not perfect, these interventions formalised protection. The implication carries into digital leadership: gentle, sincere figures still require constraints, because abuse emerges not only from malice but from asymmetry.

As a counter-example, some argue that excessive codification smothers trust and spontaneity. Smaller groups fear bureaucratic weight. A minimalist approach may seem attractive. Yet evidence suggests the opposite. When a Pacific-based parenting forum in 2022 adopted minimal oversight to preserve "organic community energy," conflicts escalated. A vulnerable member expressed distress; others responded dismissively; moderators hesitated; harm accumulated. The absence of structure did not protect spontaneity; it protected negligence. The reconciliation lies not in abandoning structure but in scaling it proportionately to community size and risk.

Throughout these claims, the motif of the lock returns: structures are not cages but safeguards. They protect the door, not restrict those living inside. And just as a locksmith evaluates weak points before designing a mechanism, leaders must examine where their communities are most vulnerable: power concentration, opaque decisions, blurred roles, unchallenged gatekeepers.

The closing movement demands a forward test. If a leader disappeared for one week, would their community know who to contact, how to report concerns, and what process would unfold? If the answer is no, then the structure relies on personality, not principle. And if structures depend on personality, the lock is already broken.

Transparent Governance: Clarity defuses suspicion

In February 2019, the board of the Royal Society of Arts in London published a detailed governance review after internal tensions about decision-making began circulating among its Fellowship. The review documented committee structures, financial controls, conflict-of-interest procedures, and oversight mechanisms with unusual specificity. Nothing sensational emerged. No scandal was uncovered. Yet the release had a concrete effect: participation in member forums rose, and grumbling about "hidden decisions" declined. The RSA's leadership noted plainly that most distrust had not come from wrongdoing but from opacity. The very act of naming the processes—every hinge and latch—restored confidence. Transparency became a stabilising force.

This scene captures a truth that digital communities encounter daily. Suspicion grows in silence. Where information flows only through informal channels or charismatic intermediaries, members begin to wonder who decides, who benefits, and who is shielded. Governance becomes folklore rather than fact. And folklore rarely flatters. The paradox is that transparency, often feared as a vulnerability, usually functions as armour. It deflects conjecture by pre-empting it.

A quiet motif runs through what follows: *the window*. Windows do not change a structure's load-bearing strength, yet they allow those outside to see inside, and those inside to look out. Transparent governance works in similar fashion. It does not weaken leadership; it makes its intentions visible.

The first major claim is that published governance reduces reputational risk more effectively than reactive clarification. To show this, consider the Wikimedia Foundation's 2020 decision to release quarterly transparency reports detailing legal requests, content takedowns, and moderation processes. Prior to publication, critics speculated about opaque deals and informal pressures. After publication, discourse shifted. People still challenged decisions, but they debated specifics rather than rumours. The named behaviour—a scheduled, structured release of information—replaced improvisation. The implication is clear: communities are less troubled by imperfect systems than by hidden ones.

A second example reinforces the point. In April 2022, the UK volunteering platform Do-it.org updated its governance portal to include board meeting summaries, financial statements, and volunteer-moderation guidelines. The move followed months of low volunteer retention and whispered concerns about mismanagement. Within two quarters, retention steadied and volunteer surveys showed reduced anxiety about organisational direction. The window had been opened; the room looked different from the outside. Transparency did not solve every issue, but it changed the interpretive atmosphere. Where information is shared predictably, suspicion loses oxygen.

A limitation complicates the picture. Too much documentation can overwhelm users rather than reassure them. The European Commission's 2018 GDPR implementation offers an example: policies ballooned in length, and compliance notices multiplied. Some communities reported confusion rather than clarity. Yet a counterexample resolves this tension. Wikipedia's transparency reports remained under ten pages, clearly structured, with charts that showed patterns over time. Brevity and clarity made the information usable. The reconciliation is instructive: transparency is not the same as data-dumping. Effective windows are clean and proportioned; they do not obstruct view with unnecessary glazing.

The second major claim concerns cost. Transparency appears burdensome, but its efficiencies outweigh its administrative load. Ambiguity consumes time. Leaders field repetitive queries, re-explain decisions, and chase misunderstandings. When a process is written, debated once, and affirmed publicly, its clarity becomes a shared reference.

To show this, take the example of the open-source design tool Figma, which in January 2021 introduced a "Community

Governance Playbook" detailing moderation hierarchy, dispute resolution steps, and criteria for feature inclusion. Prior to the playbook, the team spent significant hours responding to individual queries about why some plugins were removed or deprioritised. After publication, those hours fell markedly. Contributors cited the playbook in discussions; staff referred questioners to named sections. The organisation measured time reclaimed. The implication is structural: transparency improves efficiency precisely because it decentralises understanding.

Another named instance emerges from spiritual and educational spaces. The Quaker tradition, particularly within Britain Yearly Meeting (as documented in 2013 revisions to *Quaker Faith & Practice*), codifies governance in plain language and offers publicly available outlines of decision-making disciplines. The core behaviour is open ministry: minutes are read aloud, procedures spoken plainly, disagreements recorded honestly. Visitors often remark that the culture feels unusually trustworthy. The process is visible. The implication is quiet but profound: clarity dignifies participants by treating them as partners, not spectators.

A limitation is that transparency can provoke pushback, especially when members disagree with the revealed structures. Publishing a budget can trigger debate over allocations; releasing minutes can expose divisions. But this is not a flaw—it is a diagnostic. Debate based on facts can lead to refinement, while debate based on speculation leads only to fracture. The motif of the window returns: sunlight can reveal dust, but it also reveals what must be cleaned.

A third major claim: transparency normalises accountability and distributes it. When procedures are visible, responsibility becomes shared; when governance is hidden, responsibility centralises by default.

To illustrate, consider Mozilla's 2019 accountability experiment. The organisation trialled monthly open calls where contributors could ask senior leaders direct questions about policy, budget, and project direction. Participation surged, but more importantly, the tone of criticism changed. Contributors approached conflicts with reference to what had been discussed publicly, not with assumptions about unseen motives. Leadership's visible presence modelled accountability; contributors felt empowered to hold them to it. The implication is that visibility transforms governance from a monologue into a dialogue.

A contrasting example shows what happens in its absence. A large US-based spirituality influencer collective disintegrated in late 2020 after members discovered that funding decisions and partnership deals were negotiated privately. The collective claimed decentralisation, but no published structure confirmed it. As rumours spread, trust imploded. The leader attempted belated transparency through livestreams, but the timing was reactive. The window opened only after suspicion had hardened. The lesson is sharp: governance shared early stabilises; governance shared late appears defensive.

The fourth claim concerns emotional climate. Transparent governance does not only clarify decisions; it sets the tone of a community. People look for signals about whether leaders treat authority as stewardship or possession. The design of reporting routes, the rhythm of disclosures, the precision of minutes—all these behaviours communicate whether power is held lightly or heavily.

A named historical case strengthens the point. During the 1850s, the London-based Christian Socialist movement, influenced by thinkers like F. D. Maurice, insisted that cooperative societies publish clear records of their finances and decisions. They argued that transparency was itself a moral practice, refusing the secrecy associated with exploitative industrial firms. Their cooperatives endured longer than many competitors because members trusted the records more than personal charisma. Structures were visible. The implication carries forward: transparency signals moral posture.

The final movement leaves a test hanging. If every decision made by a leadership team were published tomorrow—budget lines, moderation calls, partnership discussions—would the community be surprised? If surprise would be widespread, the window is too small. If surprise would be mild and quickly absorbed, governance is already functioning with clarity. The unanswered question is the right one: what is the cost of remaining opaque once clarity becomes the norm expected by those you serve?

Chapter 9
Voices at the Margins

On a humid evening in July 2018, volunteers gathered in a converted classroom in Kuala Lumpur to prepare a multilingual livestream for a regional youth forum. The team spoke five languages between them. They argued, laughed, and scribbled alternates on whiteboards, not because the source text was unclear but because each word had to land with equal dignity across Malay, Tamil, Mandarin, Iban, and English. One translator, a teacher from Johor, insisted that a seemingly simple term—*community*—carried sharply different connotations depending on the dialect. The room paused. They adjusted phrasing, rearranged rhythm, and tested lines aloud. When the broadcast went live, participants across Southeast Asia commented that it "felt like being seen." Nothing spectacular happened. No viral moment, no global headline. Yet a group of young translators had quietly demonstrated a profound truth: voices at the margins do not lack depth; they lack platforms designed to hear them.

That scene illuminates a tension that runs through every digital gathering. The centre speaks effortlessly; the edges labour. Some groups must translate not only language, but context, custom, and risk. A message crafted for the majority can misfire for those whose histories carry wounds or whose identities are routinely misunderstood. The paradox is striking. Technology promises scale, yet scaled spaces amplify the privileged frequencies first. Those with quieter or more complex stories must fight to be heard—and often pay a cost to articulate themselves in the lingua franca demanded by the platform.

This chapter enters that contested terrain. It asks what it means to build communities that do not merely *tolerate* difference but cultivate it, honour it, and treat it as a resource rather than a complication. It explores how language choices signal moral imagination, how interfaith neighbourliness moderates fear, how generational teams mentor one another in public view, and how safeguarding practices determine whether the vulnerable are welcomed or exposed. The question beneath every section is the same: who is missing from the room, and why?

Language is the first frontier. Translation, as practitioners know, is never mechanical. It is interpretation layered with responsibility. A word that soothes one culture may startle another; a metaphor that delights one generation may confuse or alienate its neighbour. When communities rely on volunteers or automated tools to bridge semantic divides, they risk flattening nuance or unintentionally reinforcing hierarchies. Yet, as the Kuala Lumpur translators showed, co-creating meaning across dialects can itself become a ritual of belonging. It is not simply about accuracy. It is about shared craftsmanship and mutual recognition. A community that invites its members to shape the language of its life is a community that admits its own incompleteness and chooses to grow.

Interfaith bridges offer a parallel insight. They are rarely built on doctrinal synthesis—most groups have historical reasons to resist that—but on neighbourliness. Joint service projects, carefully bounded, demonstrate that cooperation need not collapse conviction. By working side by side on neutral ground, participants learn the cadences of one another's worlds without absorbing them wholesale. These encounters do not eliminate difference. They place difference within a frame of respect. Noise declines. Fear softens. The margins become meeting places rather than buffer zones.

Generations, too, carry their own dialects. Digital spaces often valorise speed, experimentation, and irony—the natural elements of youth. Elders bring memory, pattern recognition, and an instinct for consequences. The most fertile communities do not sideline either. They pair student leaders with mentors in co-hosted conversations, letting tempo and texture balance. When a young facilitator introduces a bold idea and an older colleague offers grounding without dampening enthusiasm, viewers experience a form of relational choreography otherwise rare online. It teaches that continuity is not the enemy of change; it is the container that allows change to endure.

Yet no expansion of voice can proceed without safeguarding. If language is the first frontier, privacy is its guardrail. Communities that do not protect the vulnerable on their platforms—survivors of abuse, young participants, those from persecuted groups—recreate the very harms they claim to resist. Anonymising stories, securing consent, moderating disclosure, and defining boundaries are not bureaucratic chores. They are acts of respect that protect the possibility of honest speech. When people know their dignity will not be traded for content, they speak more deeply. Trust gains thickness. And a community that guards its margins strengthens its centre.

A motif threads through these themes: *the margin as lens*. Looking from the edge clarifies what those at the centre no longer notice. It reveals assumptions in tone, gaps in practice, and vulnerabilities in governance. Those who inhabit the margins often see first where systems falter. When their insights shape the collective design, the whole becomes more resilient.

The introduction, then, sets the stage for a chapter concerned with more than inclusion as an abstract virtue. It is about power, language, and dignity—about who gets to define the terms of belonging and whose stories become the scaffolding of common life. The chapters before have explored formation, attention, fellowship, conflict, and governance; here the narrative widens. It asks us to listen differently, to build differently, and to consider that a community's health may be measured not by the volume of its centre but by the clarity of its margins.

What remains unresolved is the question that shadows every digital gathering: how far are we willing to redesign our spaces so that those at the edges need not strain to speak? The answer, as always, will determine who shows up—and who stays silent.

Language, Culture, and Reach

In October 2019, during a community health livestream in Nairobi, a translator named Esther Mwikali paused mid-sentence. The English term *resilience*—common in development literature—failed to align with the emotional register of the Swahili phrase she had prepared. The literal equivalent, *ustahimilivu*, carried a sense of stoic endurance rather than adaptive strength. So she tried again, drawing from Kikamba idiom: *nguvu ya kujipanga upya*—"the strength to re-prepare oneself." The chat box shifted. Viewers responded not with polite nods but with stories, questions, and clarifications in their own dialects. A single lexical decision altered the texture of the conversation. It made the teaching feel less imported and more lived. One translator's choice widened the room.

That moment illustrates a paradox at the heart of multilingual digital communities. We assume translation is a conduit, yet it is an act of authorship. A rendered sentence is not a replica of the original but a re-creation shaped by memory, culture, and judgement. Every translator carries the weight of two audiences: the speaker who seeks fidelity and the listeners who need resonance. When a word fails, meaning distorts. When a word lands, worlds meet. Five words decide. And those five words can shift the reach of an entire message.

The motif of *the hinge* emerges here—the image of a small mechanism bearing great weight. A hinge changes direction with minimal effort, yet it alters the frame of everything around it. Translation functions in precisely that way. A hinge word, a hinge phrase, a hinge metaphor: these quiet pivots decide whether a community feels addressed or merely included as an afterthought.

Translation always reveals more than it hides. When communities grow across borders, linguistic choices expose the assumptions embedded in their centre. A platform whose content defaults to one cultural code may inadvertently narrow its moral imagination. The process of translation, then, is not simply one of transport but one of discovery. It shows what the original speaker took for granted. It draws attention to the limits of one's own perspective.

The work gains clarity when we observe how translators operate in shared spaces. Consider the Global Elders Forum held in Singapore in 2016. The organisers hired simultaneous interpreters fluent in Mandarin, Malay, and Tamil, yet the conversations remained oddly detached. The interpreters were technically flawless, but the mood was transactional. During a break, a retired teacher suggested replacing literal renderings with community-curated synonyms familiar from local religious gatherings. The interpreters tried this in the next session, and participation shifted almost immediately. People nodded, interrupted, asked questions. Fidelity improved because relatability improved. The *hinge* turned.

Naming this practice—co-created translation—clarifies its significance. It is the deliberate blending of linguistic precision with cultural attunement. It acknowledges that interpretation belongs to the community, not just to the translator. The implication is profound: multilingual spaces are healthiest when members help shape their own linguistic bridges. When translation becomes collective, trust grows measurable. A 2021 ethnographic study by the Asia Foundation documented that communities using decentralised translation teams saw a 40 per cent rise in cross-dialect participation (Asia Foundation, 2021). People speak more when they recognise themselves in the shared vocabulary.

Yet limitations remain. Automated tools still dominate much online discourse. They excel in speed but falter in texture. Machine-generated captions can misread idiom, tone, or context, particularly for minority dialects. A 2022 audit by Masakhane, the African NLP consortium, reported accuracy gaps of up to 30 per cent between major and regional languages. These tools democratise access, but they also risk imposing a linguistic hierarchy in which some voices appear polished while others seem fragmented or incoherent. The counter-example is real. But reconciliation is possible. Communities can pair automation with human correction, treating machines as first drafts rather than final arbiters. When volunteers revise automated captions—highlighting nuance, adjusting idiom—they resist the homogenising pressure of dominant-language norms.

The core of the issue is not technology but posture. Translation is a behavioural practice before it is a technical one. It demands the discipline to slow down, to enquire, to measure the fit between word and world. It requires the humility to accept that one's own phrasing may not travel cleanly. That humility is visible in small decisions: a community leader asking members which terms feel dignifying; a moderator adjusting tone after noticing discomfort; a translator choosing a metaphor drawn from a listener's landscape rather than the speaker's library. These decisions accumulate. They form the hinge-work of trust.

Culture shapes that hinge-work more than any algorithm. A message framed around individual achievement may resonate strongly in London but land awkwardly in Jakarta, where collective identity holds greater weight. A teaching on forgiveness using courtroom metaphors may energise American audiences but confuse participants from regions where family arbitration, not legal procedure, defines reconciliation. Effective leaders study these patterns. They commit to translation not as a final step but as an embedded design principle.

Two examples illustrate the stakes. In 2017, a youth organisation in Manila adapted a mental health curriculum originally drafted in California. Instead of translating it verbatim, they rewrote its key metaphors using Filipino narratives of *bayanihan*—collective uplift. Participation doubled. The content softened because the surrounding culture softened it. A year later, a European NGO attempted a similar localisation in Guatemala but failed to consult community elders. Their literal translation preserved accuracy but lost dignity. Engagement declined. The limitation was not linguistic; it was relational. The hinge refused to turn.

These cases remind us that translation is a negotiation of power. Whose words are treated as standard? Whose metaphors are considered universal? Communities that centre dominant languages without scrutiny risk reinforcing structural imbalances. Yet those that invite marginal voices to co-author shared vocabulary reconfigure the power map. They loosen the grip of the centre, allowing the margins to define meaning rather than merely adapt to it.

A recurring question surfaces: what does it mean for a digital community to sound like all of its members rather than merely echo its founders? The answer lies in patterns of behaviour. Leaders who routinely solicit feedback in multiple languages, publish glossaries shaped by community revision, or rotate translation duties send a clear signal: this space belongs to many histories, not one. That signal does more than broaden reach. It recalibrates identity. A community that speaks in many registers becomes more agile, more honest, and more capable of learning.

The hinge motif returns as we approach the tension underpinning the subchapter. If translation is interpretation, and interpretation is power, how do leaders design processes that honour multiplicity without dissolving coherence? The risk is real. Too much dispersion can fragment meaning; too little can silence difference. The challenge lies in holding both commitments simultaneously: clarity without uniformity, unity without erasure.

The question remains unresolved by design. It is the forward test for any community crossing linguistic borders. Which words will you let your people remake? Which metaphors will you retire? Which idioms will you adopt, not because they are familiar to you, but because they welcome someone who has strained too long to understand?

Everything turns on the hinge.

Interfaith Bridges: Neighbourliness beats noise

On 14 December 2006, in Kaduna, northern Nigeria, an unusual scene unfolded outside the ruins of a market stall destroyed in the previous week's clashes. Christian and Muslim youth—members of the Interfaith Mediation Centre founded by Imam Muhammad Ashafa and Pastor James Wuye—worked side by side to rebuild a small carpenter's shop. Hammering replaced shouting; shared labour drowned the rhetoric that had fuelled riot. Journalists expected a press conference. The volunteers offered tea instead. No statements, no slogans, no attempts at theological synthesis—just neighbours repairing what their neighbours had lost. By dusk, the shop stood again. The violence did not vanish, but that day's work created a hinge in the city's story: a tiny pivot where cooperation replaced spectacle. Five hours changed something that five years of conferences had not.

The paradox of interfaith engagement is stark. Why do the conversations with the most doctrinal weight so often produce the least human warmth, while the smallest acts—painting a fence, distributing food, clearing rubble—generate trust that formal dialogue fails to achieve? The question remains unresolved because the answer resists abstraction. Trust grows visible. It grows measurable. It grows in the mundane. And it grows precisely when groups respect their boundaries rather than erasing them.

Interfaith work has long been haunted by suspicion. Communities fear dilution, co-option, or quiet pressure to conform. Leaders worry that genuine engagement risks drifting into syncretism. But the Kaduna moment—one among many—shows a different route. Neighbourliness, not noise: cooperation without collapse of identity. Joint work with clear limits. Friendship that does not require doctrinal merging. The motif of *the table* emerges here: a simple surface where difference sits without demanding resolution. A table can hold many items without blending them. That quiet image threads through every effective interfaith space.

The core claim is simple: shared action, not shared dogma, is the most durable engine of interfaith trust. The evidence spans continents. In 2011, the "Better Together" campaign launched by the Interfaith Youth Core in Chicago invited university students from Christian, Muslim, Jewish, and secular backgrounds to collaborate on local service projects. The organisation measured outcomes carefully: campuses that ran sustained, mixed-faith volunteer programmes recorded a 27 per cent rise in students reporting "high trust" in peers of other religions (IFYC, 2014). Trust, again, became measurable not through the eloquence of dialogue but through the rhythm of joint labour—packing meals, clearing gardens, tutoring children. The table widened.

The pattern holds historically as well. In 1994, during the fragile years following the Oslo Accords, Jewish and Arab medical teams at Hadassah Hospital in Jerusalem coordinated emergency care during a bus bombing. Their cooperation was not designed as interfaith dialogue; it was professional duty. Yet that event later informed joint training sessions that continued long after negotiations collapsed. A hospital ward became a civic classroom. The table held.

Showing the pattern is not enough; naming it clarifies its force. This is *practical neighbourliness*—a model grounded in shared action rather than shared doctrine. It recognises the gravitational pull of difference and chooses to work with it, not against it. Practical neighbourliness avoids the two failures common in interfaith life: turning engagement into public performance, or stripping identities so thin that the collaboration becomes hollow. Instead, it aligns purpose with honesty: let us work together precisely because we are not the same.

The implication is significant. When interfaith work removes its performative veneer, communities commit more deeply to their own integrity. People speak more plainly. Suspicion decreases because stakes become clearer. The Muslim carpenter in Kaduna understood that the Christian volunteers were not trying to convert him; they were trying to repair what violence had broken. The Christians understood the same. That clarity enabled cooperation.

Yet limitations exist, and they must be named without sentimentality. Not all interfaith spaces succeed. Some collapse under the weight of unresolved grievances. A striking counter-example comes from the 2015 joint summit in Colombo, where Buddhist and Muslim leaders attempted to host a shared workshop on religious nationalism. Tensions escalated quickly. Delegates walked out. Critics mocked the event as naïve. But analysis later revealed the root issue: the meeting blurred too many theological and political lines without establishing boundaries first. The table wobbled because the legs were weak.

How do we reconcile this limitation with the earlier successes? By recognising that neighbourliness requires structure. Effective interfaith engagement thrives when boundaries are not merely acknowledged but designed. The most resilient models include defined aims, clear exclusions, and explicit respect for doctrinal differences. They commit to working *alongside*, not *through*. They do not attempt to flatten conflict. They attempt to contain it. That containment creates space for dignity.

Structure appears again in Singapore's 2020 "Faiths for the City" initiative. The organisers crafted joint service projects—elderly care, environmental clean-ups—but deliberately prohibited joint liturgies, shared prayers, or blended rituals. Each group maintained its theological integrity. Yet participants ate together, travelled together, and compared practical challenges of serving ageing populations. The boundaries strengthened the trust. The table stayed balanced because its edges were firm.

Interfaith engagement is not merely an exercise in politeness. It is a test of a community's capacity for moral imagination. Can one respect another's sacred commitments while defending one's own? Can one disagree sharply on metaphysics yet join hands to repair a world that requires repair regardless of doctrine? These questions gain urgency in digital spaces, where proximity is instantaneous but depth is scarce.

Online, interfaith engagement easily degrades into spectacle: panels that function as branding; comment threads that mimic debate but generate little insight; curated displays of harmony that collapse under scrutiny. Noise rises. Substance diminishes. The table vanishes beneath the clutter.

Yet digital spaces also offer opportunities that physical ones cannot. The "Faithful Neighbours Network" launched in Manchester in 2021 demonstrates this potential. Local leaders held asynchronous Q&A sessions where members submitted questions about one another's traditions. Moderators paired each question with a concise, community-approved response in plain language, avoiding commentary on contentious doctrinal claims. Participation increased because expectations were explicit. Hard questions were not avoided; they were honoured within defined boundaries. The network then launched small interfaith task groups to support refugee resettlement. Not one session attempted to merge beliefs. The table remained recognisable, and therefore trustworthy.

Behaviour reveals the deeper pattern. In every successful case, leaders chose actions that slowed escalation and strengthened clarity. They committed to ground rules: no proselytising, no rhetorical ambushes, no attempts to "bridge" theological gaps that tradition holds as non-negotiable. Participants observed pace. They listened before speaking. They measured tone. They let silence play its part.

These behaviours matter. They are metrics of neighbourliness, not sentiment.

The tension running through this subchapter is unavoidable. Interfaith engagement demands two commitments that seem incompatible: robust identity and genuine cooperation. The risk of dilution exists. So does the risk of fragmentation. Communities must choose which concessions are permissible and which would betray their core. These decisions cannot be outsourced. They must be owned.

As we return to the motif of *the table*, the unresolved question sharpens. What shape must a shared table take so that no participant feels trapped, compromised, or tokenised? How wide can the table extend before its centre collapses? And what happens when a community required to sit at that table has been wounded too many times to trust the invitation?

Interfaith bridges hold only when their builders resist the lure of noise. Neighbourliness asks less and offers more. It does not promise agreement. It promises dignity. And the next decision for any leader is clear: which concrete task, offered with clear boundaries and shared purpose, will become the next table where strangers discover they need not become similar in order to become allies?

Youth Voices and Elders: Generational teams balance energy and wisdom

When the Archbishop of Canterbury hosted the Lambeth Youth Summit in London in July 2022, observers expected formality: keynote speeches, polite panels, predictable questions. Instead, the opening session turned the room on its axis. A nineteen-year-old delegate from Nairobi asked why senior leaders still designed programmes "for the youth" rather than "with the youth," and an eighty-year-old priest beside her nodded before anyone else did. The applause that followed was not the noisy enthusiasm of a conference crowd but the steady, resonant approval of participants recognising a shift. The summit ended three days later with an agreement that future gatherings would be co-chaired by one youth representative and one elder. It was a modest administrative change. It altered the dynamics inside the room immediately.

A paradox haunts every digital community that aspires to serve more than one generation. Younger members generate momentum; older members supply ballast. Too much energy and the space veers into chaos. Too much caution and the room calcifies. The question is therefore precise: how do communities design structures where the sharp pace of youth and the slow depth of elders do not compete, but complete? The answer resists clichés about harmony. It is architectural. It must be measured in visible behaviours—the frequency of intergenerational exchanges, the quality of shared decision-making, the durability of projects stewarded by teams rather than age-defined blocs.

The motif that threads through this subchapter is *the relay*: the baton passed, not thrown; the race run together rather than consecutively. In effective generational teams, leadership is not transferred once but circulated repeatedly. Momentum builds when the baton keeps moving. The relay image returns often because it captures the core truth: wisdom without energy stalls; energy without wisdom spills.

The visible evidence for intergenerational collaboration emerges most clearly when communities commit to co-hosting, co-teaching, and co-moderating. The Lambeth Youth Summit's experiment did not end in the conference hall. One of its delegates, Rev Canon Mpho Tutu van Furth, invited a group of youth leaders to co-design an online liturgy series later that year. Metrics tracked by her team showed that livestream engagement increased by 18 per cent over six weeks, and the retention rate held unusually steady. These numbers matter not because they demonstrate reach but because they reveal behaviour: participants stayed because the dynamic between youth and elders modelled shared authority rather than symbolic inclusion. The relay worked.

A second example comes from the American Friends Service Committee's 2018 "Youth and Elders for Justice" programme in Philadelphia. The organisers paired high-school students with long-time civil rights activists to document neighbourhood histories. The students conducted interviews, edited footage, and led the digital publication. The elders supplied context, memory, and the slow precision of lived experience. The outcome—an online archive now used by local schools—was less important than the process that produced it. Trust became visible in the choices both sides made: students accepting editorial feedback; elders adjusting to unfamiliar technologies. Each group altered pace to match the other. The baton stayed in motion.

Yet not all intergenerational initiatives succeed. A well-documented counter-example emerges from the 2010 launch of "Generations Connect," an EU-funded online forum intended to foster debate across age groups. Despite generous resources, the project stalled within nine months. Younger participants complained that moderators, many of whom were retired professionals, responded with slow, essay-length comments that smothered conversation. Elders felt dismissed by what they perceived as superficial reactions from students. The forum recorded steep decline: engagement dropped by 70 per cent between February and October 2010. The baton was dropped because the pacing rules were unclear. Neither group adjusted its stride.

Reconciling this limitation requires naming a principle: intergenerational work fails not because generations differ but because expectations differ. Communities that succeed establish pace agreements. They design formats that honour both brevity and depth. They measure interaction frequency and balance it with structured pauses. They show, through concrete scheduling, that both energy and wisdom matter. This is not romantic rhetoric. It is operational clarity.

Digital communities, in particular, feel generational tension acutely because digital time is asymmetric. Younger members operate in rapid cycles—memetic frames, short-form clips, instantaneous commentary. Older members tend towards slower cycles—long-form reflections, careful revisions, considered replies. The friction arises when these cycles collide without structure. A youth-led discussion might move through five topics in one hour. An elder might want to stay with one question for a week. Without coordination, both groups feel unheard.

Communities that recognise *the relay* motif craft formats that temper these cycles rather than erase them. Co-hosted live streams provide a case study. When a student leader shapes the opening fifteen minutes with a crisp narrative and an elder frames the final fifteen with reflection, the contrast becomes complementary. Observers witness pace calibrated rather than imposed. The baton passes clearly between segments. The intergenerational team becomes a visible symbol of mutual respect.

The implication extends beyond programming. Generational teams create accountability for content quality. Younger leaders, for example, often identify blind spots in digital accessibility—missing captions, cluttered interfaces, outdated language. Elders identify ethical hazards—privacy oversights, over-promising claims, or subtle shifts in community norms that risk harm. When decisions are made together, risk decreases and care increases. You can measure this: communities with defined intergenerational councils report fewer crisis escalations because more perspectives are embedded upstream rather than consulted downstream.

Historical patterns reinforce the case. The Quaker movement's tradition of "elders and youth ministers" in the eighteenth century illustrates how centuries-old structures placed young speakers under the guidance of seasoned companions during public ministry. These pairings were not hierarchical; they were reciprocal. Young ministers travelled widely, carrying intense conviction; elders carried steadiness and discernment. Letters from the period record how these teams prevented burnout and improved doctrinal clarity (Friends Historical Society, 1922). The relay again: the baton passed deliberately, never abandoned.

But the digital age poses a new challenge. It is easy for communities to mistake visibility for voice. Young people might appear frequently in content yet hold little real influence over governance. Elders might hold authority but remain invisible, making their guidance abstract rather than embodied. Communities must therefore distinguish representation from participation. Representation shows presence. Participation shows power. Generational teams only flourish when both groups share real decision-making. The baton must be held, not merely touched.

One risk persists: tokenism. Inviting a youth representative into a leadership meeting without adjusting meeting structures—pace, agenda, terminology—creates symbolic inclusion with no substantive effect. Conversely, sidelining elders to occasional advisory roles deprives the community of depth and memory. The limitation here is easy to diagnose but harder to repair. The remedy lies in designing spaces where each generation's strengths appear through visible actions: youth setting timeframes, elders setting guardrails; youth proposing experiments, elders assessing consequences; youth naming trends, elders mapping patterns. The table becomes a workshop rather than a showcase.

The relay motif returns when discussing conflict. Intergenerational friction is not a sign of failure. It is a sign of life. Communities with only one tempo stagnate. Communities with two tempos clash before they learn to coordinate. The question is whether the baton survives the clash. When youth feel dismissed, they disengage. When elders feel bypassed, they withdraw. Repair requires both groups to adjust pace long enough to understand the other's rhythm.

Co-led mentoring circles offer one solution. In 2020, a community arts centre in Glasgow piloted an intergenerational mentorship scheme during the pandemic. Sessions alternated between rapid creative exercises led by young participants and reflective discussion led by older facilitators. Feedback surveys revealed a key pattern: participants reported the highest sense of connection when the baton passed mid-session rather than between sessions. The alternation of tempo within a single hour created coherence. The relay held.

The unresolved tension remains. How does a community maintain generational balance when crises demand speed? Emergencies compress time. Youth will respond faster. Elders will advise caution. Both instincts are valuable. But what happens when acting quickly risks long-term damage, and acting slowly risks losing the moment? Which hand should hold the baton then?

Communities that navigate this tension resist the temptation to sideline one group. They slow enough to listen, accelerate enough to act, and leave enough ambiguity to learn. The next step is not theoretical. It is concrete: who holds the baton in your next decision, and who must be invited to take it next so that energy and wisdom do not drift into separate lanes?

Safeguarding Vulnerable Communities: Privacy and consent are paramount

In May 2019, the Independent Inquiry into Child Sexual Abuse (IICSA) in London released a report detailing how several organisations had published survivor testimonies without securing explicit, informed consent. One case involved a support charity in Birmingham that shared anonymised case summaries in a fundraising newsletter; yet investigators found that two survivors could identify themselves from the contextual details. The consequences were immediate. The charity suspended its digital storytelling programme, apologised publicly, and rewrote its governance framework within six months. The harm was not born of malice but of a structural failure to understand that *privacy is relational*: the storyteller's world, not the institution's assumptions, defines what counts as identifiable. The lesson was stark. Good intentions do not shield vulnerable people. Precision does.

The paradox is unsettling. Digital communities claim that stories shape understanding, yet the act of telling a story can expose the very people it seeks to protect. How does a community teach well when the audience's learning must never come at the price of an individual's safety? The tension becomes sharper when the community stretches across borders, where privacy laws diverge and cultural expectations about disclosure shift. A story that feels safely anonymised in one city can become traceable in another. What seems like harmless detail may become a breadcrumb trail. Consent is therefore not an administrative form but a living agreement shaped by context, capacity, and control.

A motif threads through this subchapter: *the closed door*. It signals dignity and the right to choose who enters a story, when, and in what form. Communities that safeguard well learn to respect the closed door even when the room behind it holds teaching value. They slow down before opening anything. They ask before crossing thresholds.

They measure not how compelling a narrative is but how protected the person at its centre remains.

The central claim is visible when communities commit to privacy-by-design rather than privacy-by-apology. The IICSA case shows the cost of reactive safeguarding. A contrasting example demonstrates an alternative. In 2021, the Rape Crisis Scotland helpline launched a digital awareness campaign based entirely on composite narratives crafted from multiple cases. The organisation's designers worked with advocates to identify risk markers—geography, family structure, workplace patterns—and intentionally blurred or removed them. The campaign's metric of success was not reach but zero breaches. After twelve months, an external audit confirmed that no individual could be plausibly identified. The relay between survivor experience and public education remained intact because the closed door stayed closed.

A second example emerges from Médecins Sans Frontières (MSF) during its 2014 Ebola response work in Monrovia. Field teams collected testimonies to counter misinformation spreading through local radio. But MSF implemented a protocol requiring at least two layers of consent: first, agreement to speak; second, agreement to share. Survivors could withdraw at any stage. A 2015 internal review reported that 27 per cent of participants chose to retract consent during review, often after realising how easily neighbours might recognise contextual details. MSF honoured every withdrawal. The educational content remained effective because the process treated consent as iterative. The closed door could be opened only from the inside.

Yet limitations remain. Not all safeguarding efforts succeed, even when organisations act honourably. A credible counter-example comes from a 2020 community mental-health forum in Toronto, designed to allow anonymous peer support. Moderators removed usernames and blurred avatars in archived discussions, believing anonymity had been achieved. But researchers later found that conversational patterns—recurring jokes, references to local landmarks, specific medication histories—created indirect identifiers. A small number of users were recognised by acquaintances. The forum tightened its anonymisation protocols, but the breach had occurred. This failure illustrates a hard truth: full anonymity can be undermined by the richness of human detail. The closed door may have tiny gaps that outsiders can peer through.

Reconciling this limitation requires precision rather than despair. Communities must acknowledge that anonymity is not a single switch but a layered system. They must minimise identifiable texture without amputating humanity. They must decide which details are pedagogically essential and which are ornamental. They must recognise that the storyteller's risk threshold—not the moderator's guess—defines the acceptable boundary. The closed door can hold if the frame is built with care.

Digital environments complicate safeguarding because the speed of information flow accelerates harm. A single screenshot can escape within seconds. A private chat can circulate far beyond its intended audience. This means privacy protocols must be measured not only in rules but in behaviours: moderators intervening early; members reporting breaches; leaders modelling restraint by withholding sensitive content even when the educational impulse tempts them to share. Safeguarding is therefore not an abstract value but a set of visible decisions taken repeatedly.

The principle of consent must be expanded beyond legal compliance to meaningful comprehension. In multilingual communities, translation can distort risk. Consent obtained in English may conceal nuances lost when the content circulates in Arabic or Tagalog. Consider the approach used by the International Refugee Assistance Project (IRAP) in 2017 when it gathered testimonies from Syrian families resettled in Berlin. The team employed community translators who clarified not only vocabulary but implications—how a detail might travel, how honour dynamics might shift risk perception within extended families. IRAP treated translators as cultural sentinels, not mechanical intermediaries. The closed door remained guarded in every language.

A parallel can be seen in the UK's domestic abuse sector. Women's Aid, in its 2018 digital storytelling guidelines, required facilitators to implement a "24-hour reconsideration window" after survivors viewed edited content. This window was not bureaucratic padding;

it reflected an empirical insight from trauma research that cognitive processing improves with time. Survivors often reduced or altered the details they wanted shared once the emotional intensity subsided. This practice did not dilute narratives. It strengthened them by aligning storytelling with autonomy.

But safeguarding is not solely about protecting survivors. It includes shielding vulnerable contributors—young people, elders, migrants, refugees—from pressures they may not recognise. Youth may agree to share stories without understanding long-term digital persistence. Elders may disclose more than they intend because they assume online spaces behave like small in-person rooms. Migrants may fear consequences from authorities or family. Communities must therefore measure consent not by the existence of a signature but by the contributor's actual ability to withdraw, revise, or veto.

The closed door motif reappears in governance. Communities require structures that prevent harm rather than merely respond to it. This means independent safeguarding teams rather than informal volunteer moderators; published protocols rather than vague norms; clear escalation pathways rather than improvised reactions. Transparency strengthens privacy because it sets predictable expectations. When members know who holds their stories and how those stories are handled, suspicion diminishes.

A challenge persists when global communities operate across jurisdictions. The EU's GDPR treats health data as highly sensitive; the US patchwork of laws does not. In India, proposed data protection legislation has shifted several times. A community spanning London, Nairobi, and Mumbai cannot rely on national frameworks alone. It must adopt the highest common standard. This choice is not ideological. It is a practical shield. The closed door must be reinforced at its weakest hinge.

A further tension emerges between teaching and safeguarding. Stories illuminate moral questions. They reveal patterns. They carry weight. But when does an illustrative narrative risk becoming exploitative? Communities must ask: is this detail essential to understanding, or merely emotive? Does the story teach because it is dramatic, or because its insight is transferable? Removing unnecessary specificity is not a dilution but an act of honour. Memory can remain intact while identifiers vanish.

Some communities adopt composite narratives to preserve insight without exposing individuals. This technique succeeds when implemented rigorously. It fails when composite characters become too realistic, accidentally mirroring one real person's circumstances. Safeguarding requires disciplined fictionalisation: merging timelines, shifting locations, altering roles. The goal is not deception but protection. The closed door stays shut while the lesson walks freely.

The final tension touches power. Safeguarding can become paternalistic if leaders assume they always know best. Conversely, communities that avoid firm boundaries in the name of empowerment risk abandoning vulnerable members. The challenge is therefore relational: how to create structures that protect without smothering, that guard without infantilising. Consent becomes dialogue, not decree.

The unresolved question remains. As digital communities expand, stories will continue to shape understanding. But who decides which stories may enter the teaching space? Who checks that the closed door remains shut? And when the educational value feels compelling, will the community pause long enough to ask whether it is compelling enough to warrant crossing the threshold at all?

Chapter 10
A Rule of Life for the Feed

The night before he deleted his channels, the American pastor and writer Eugene Peterson—widely known for *The Message* translation of the Bible—was asked in a 2015 interview why he had stepped back from public visibility at the height of his influence. The interviewer expected a reference to exhaustion or criticism. Peterson instead spoke of rhythm. He described how the pace of digital attention had begun to distort his inner life, pulling him into "performances of immediacy" rather than the slower habits that had sustained his vocation for decades. He felt himself becoming reactive. "I needed to recover a way of living," he said quietly. What startled listeners was not the decision to pause but the clarity with which he recognised its spiritual and moral necessity long before a scandal or crisis forced the question. He was not retreating; he was recalibrating.

This tension—between the speed of the feed and the slower, sturdier movements of a meaningful life—sits at the heart of the chapter ahead. Many creators assume that the pressures of visibility demand constant output. Yet the digital environments that reward immediacy often corrode the very qualities audiences hunger for: depth, coherence, steadiness, presence. The paradox grows sharper each year. Our platforms run faster; our souls do not. A creator may gain followers through relentless production, but without an anchored rhythm of life, the cost eventually appears: burnout disguised as productivity, performative authenticity masquerading as care, and communities shaped more by volatility than by wisdom. If earlier chapters of this book traced the dynamics of attention, belonging, and conflict in digital spaces, this one steps back to ask a prior and more foundational question: how does a leader live in such a space without losing their centre?

History offers an unexpected lens. Long before uploads and livestreams, monastic communities across the Mediterranean and northern Europe understood that influence without discipline is dangerous. The Rule of St Benedict, written around 530 CE, was not composed as a strategic document; it was a way of life. It structured prayer, labour, study, conflict, rest, and leadership with unembarrassed specificity. Crucially, it insisted that a community's flourishing could not be detached from the interior life of the one who guided it. In Benedict's language, stability and mutual accountability mattered as much as talent or charisma. The past rarely maps neatly onto the present, yet the principle endures: pace is not solved by productivity tools but by a lived pattern that precedes and governs public action.

This chapter concerns itself with that pattern. Not as nostalgia, nor as a rejection of digital culture, but as a rigorous and necessary response to it. A "Rule of Life" for creators is not a branded slogan; it is a set of commitments that shape the one who teaches before they teach anyone else. It answers questions that most platforms never ask: What nourishes you? What depletes you? Who has permission to tell you you're drifting? What fruit do you long to see in your community—fruit that cannot be counted in views or likes? And how will you recognise when your voice must soften, pause, or pass into new hands?

Consider the quiet power of small oversight circles—those groups of two or three who read drafts, test tone, notice emotional fatigue, ask inconvenient questions about motive, and remind creators that they are accountable to more than metrics. Their value lies not in surveillance but in companionship: the simple insistence that no one should carry a public platform alone. At their best, these circles function like the spiritual friends whose presence steadies a leader's imagination and closes the gap between what they profess and how they live. They create a counterpoint to the drift that occurs when a single voice speaks into a vacuum of applause or hostility.

Yet this chapter reaches further. It presses the question of measurement itself. The platforms have their numbers, but communities have stories. Reconciliations achieved after months of tension. Acts of service initiated quietly by members who once lurked on the margins. Small but decisive shifts in a group's capacity to listen. These metrics require patience to surface and humility to trust; they ask leaders to trade immediacy for substance. They also resist the emotional exploitation that can accompany impact narratives. Where a strategy team might spotlight a moving testimonial, a Rule of Life cautions the leader to protect the storyteller first, even at the cost of promotional clarity.

The thread of seasons runs through what follows. Every digital creator faces moments when continuity becomes harm: when weariness accumulates; when a community needs a new register or a new guide; when legacy demands letting go. Planned sabbaticals and transparent succession plans are not signs of frailty but of stewardship. They honour the principle that influence is temporary and communal wellbeing long outlives any single voice. A Rule of Life helps leaders recognise not only when to speak but when to fall silent; not only how to innovate but how to end well.

Through these lenses—rhythm, accountability, discernment, seasonality—the chapter invites a sober rethinking of what it means to lead online. It resists the modern myth that digital visibility requires self-erasure, and it challenges the equally common myth that good intentions guarantee good outcomes. Instead, it proposes a framework in which creators cultivate a life sturdy enough to bear the weight of influence: a life paced by rest, strengthened by companions, measured by fruit that algorithms cannot see, and ordered by the humility to step aside when the time comes.

The final pages will not offer quick fixes. They will offer something sterner and more generative: a vision of leadership that grows from coherence rather than spectacle, from depth rather than velocity. The invitation is simple but demanding. Before you shape the feed, shape yourself. And before you ask others to follow, decide the kind of life you are willing to live.

A Rule of Life for Creators: Write a lived rule before a content strategy

In January 1941, in a small cell at St John's Abbey in Collegeville, Minnesota, the Benedictine monk Virgil Michel wrote that a community "is shaped first by the rhythm of its life, not by the brilliance of its speech." His notes from that winter show no concern with public influence; instead, they record waking hours, shared meals, silence at dusk, and the sequence of prayers that framed each day. Michel believed these ordinary habits formed a leader's imagination far more deeply than any public address. Decades later, scholars credit this rhythm-focused approach with sustaining the abbey through periods of cultural upheaval and wartime strain. The stability did not emerge from strategy. It emerged from a lived rule.

That contrast—between the hidden life that shapes a person and the visible output that others consume—remains one of the most neglected tensions in digital leadership. A creator might refine scripts, polish schedules, and build publishing systems, yet still operate from a life that is hurried, hollow, or reactive. The mismatch becomes visible in subtle ways: tone that grows brittle, judgement that becomes impulsive, and communities that mirror their leader's exhaustion rather than their wisdom. The platforms reward speed. A rule of life trains steadiness. One asks for immediate engagement metrics; the other insists on practices that no metric can capture. The feed moves fast. Your life must not.

Creators often assume that growth demands a content strategy, but strategy without a rule is a brittle scaffolding. The motif that threads through this chapter—the quiet image of a trellis—helps clarify the point. A trellis does not produce fruit; it holds the plant so it may grow in the right direction. In the same way, a rule of life supports the inner structures that keep a creator's voice honest, humane, and sane. Remove the trellis and the plant sprawls. Remove the rule and the creator's intention sprawls with it: ideas spread thin, motives blur, and the feed dictates pace rather than principle. The trellis motif will return because it captures the stakes with unusual clarity.

To understand what a rule of life might mean for digital creators, it helps to begin with a concrete pattern. In 2020, the theologian and podcaster Kate Bowler publicly shared that her production rhythm was anchored—quite literally—in a paper schedule taped to her desk: half an hour of morning reading, fifteen minutes of handwritten prayer, a set time for correspondence, a three-hour block for writing, and a strict boundary around evenings with her family. Though Bowler's platform grew rapidly, she refused to allow the feed to set her hours. Her team later noted that this simple rule insulated their work from algorithmic volatility; when a video unexpectedly went viral, Bowler declined to alter her established rhythm. The result was not slower growth but steadier presence.

Show, then name, then explain. What Bowler modelled is what monastic and scholarly traditions have long called rule-before-work: the principle that the leader's life must be ordered before their speech can carry weight. Intellectual labour, teaching, and community leadership are not free-floating activities; they depend on a daily pattern that nourishes the one who performs them. For creators, this might include prayer or reflection, but it also encompasses rest hours, study windows, regular service outside the platform, and non-negotiable time in which the leader is unavailable for public commentary. Without these anchors, the feed becomes the unseen master, setting expectations that the body and mind cannot sustain. The implication is sharp: if your life has no rule, your content is ruled by forces you do not name.

A second example makes the dynamic even clearer. In 2022, the British historian Sathnam Sanghera described the discipline he adopted while writing *Empireland*: scheduled reading every morning, research documents organised by theme rather than algorithmic news cycles, and a weekly conversation with two trusted friends who asked whether his arguments were drifting into reaction rather than reason. Sanghera has said that this rhythm protected him from the whiplash of political commentary on Twitter, where pressure to respond rapidly could have distorted his work. His book's eventual impact—becoming a Sunday Times bestseller—was rooted not in public engagement but in a rule that stabilised his thinking long before publication.

These examples show rule-before-output, yet they also reveal a limitation. A rule of life can appear rigid or self-protective if it calcifies into a system that excludes responsiveness or compassion. There are moments when creators must break routine to address urgent events or support a community experiencing shock. During the Manchester Arena attack in May 2017, several local faith leaders abandoned their scheduled content plans and met physically with affected families, providing care long before issuing public statements. Their deviation from routine did not violate a rule of life; it fulfilled it. The rule exists to serve people, not to bind compassion.

Reconciliation of principle and flexibility is essential: the trellis holds the plant, but it must not choke it.

The heart of a creator's rule lies in decisions shaped by commitment rather than momentum. If a rule includes weekly study, the visible behaviour is not the idea of "depth" but the open book on the desk, the calendar block that protects it, and the willingness to decline a trending collaboration to preserve that time. If a rule includes service, the visible behaviour may be two hours each week in a local food bank or mentoring young creators whose work rarely gets attention. These actions form the leader's moral imagination, preventing their voice from being shaped solely by visibility. Metrics help measure reach; habits measure character.

One of the quietest yet most transformative elements of a rule is rest. Not the vague notion of "self-care" but measured, scheduled hours in which publishing ceases and consumption slows. The neuroscientist Matthew Walker (University of California, 2017) has shown that regular sleep cycles improve emotional regulation and cognitive clarity—capacities essential for creators whose words travel further than intended. A creator who routinely posts late at night, driven by anxiety or haste, signals that their life is governed by the feed. A rule that includes rest interrupts this pattern. The motif of the trellis returns here: rest is one of its core beams, holding the weight of everything else.

Yet the most overlooked component of a creator's rule is companionship. Many digital leaders operate alone, believing solitude protects focus or authenticity. In practice, solitary creators often drift into extremes: overwork, oversharing, or overconfidence. Accountability circles—small, trusted groups who meet regularly to ask about wellbeing, motive, and tone—ground the leader in real relationships rather than parasocial projections. In 2018, the writer Debie Thomas described how her small trio of readers kept her honest as she wrote about faith and trauma, ensuring she did not exploit her own history for impact. Their questions shaped the cadence of her work, preventing both sensationalism and self-erasure. The implication is clear: a rule of life requires people, not just principles.

The counter-example here is equally instructive. Some creators form accountability circles that function as fan clubs rather than safeguards. When a group depends socially or financially on the creator, accountability evaporates. The names need not be listed; recent public failures across media, religion, and activism show how insulated leaders lose sight of reality. The reconciliation lies in the structure: companions must be independent enough to challenge, close enough to care, and willing to ask questions the audience never will. A rule of life must include oversight that strengthens, not flatters.

As the chapter moves deeper into implications, a subtle shift emerges: a rule is not simply a defensive shield against exhaustion or notoriety; it is a generative engine for coherence. When prayer or quiet reflection sits before publication, the creator's tone typically softens. When study precedes commentary, accuracy improves. When service precedes branding, communities sense the difference. When rest sits before response, reactions become measured rather than impulsive. The rule shapes the person. The person shapes the content. The content shapes the community. And the community, in turn, shapes culture.

The trellis motif tightens the argument further. A rule is not a cage. It is a frame that channels growth. In horticulture, gardeners prune vines not to diminish them but to produce fruit. Creators often assume that pruning—reducing output, narrowing focus, or declining opportunities—will harm reach. Yet pruning can heighten clarity. The writer Marilynne Robinson once said in a 2014 lecture at Yale that "simplicity is an act of reverence." For creators, simplicity in rhythm can become an act of reverence toward the people they serve: a commitment to speak only from what is lived, not merely researched or improvised.

This raises the chapter's unresolved question, the one that lingers beneath every paragraph: what rule shapes your life before you speak into the lives of others? The feed will not answer it for you. The platforms cannot supply it. The community cannot impose it. Only the creator can commit to a pattern that steadies motive, deepens substance, and limits excess. That commitment carries a cost. It demands fewer late-night uploads, fewer reactive posts, more hours away from screens, and a willingness to let the trellis hold what ambition cannot.

The tension remains. How firm should a rule be before it becomes inflexible? How open should a creator remain before they become unmoored? How will they know when the trellis needs strengthening—or when it needs repair? These questions cannot be resolved by metrics or by strategy. They must be lived. And their answers will shape not only the creator's future but the communities that gather, day after day, around the words they offer.

Team and Accountability: Lone voices drift

In February 2010, the *Boston Globe* published an interview with the veteran editor Walter Robinson, reflecting on why the Spotlight team's investigative reporting had endured when other newsrooms faltered. He credited not brilliance but structure: every major story passed through a small circle of colleagues who challenged assumptions, examined tone, and asked whether the reporting served the public rather than personal ambition. The method was slow and occasionally uncomfortable, yet it produced work that reshaped institutions across Massachusetts and beyond. Robinson insisted that no journalist, however experienced, could see their own blind spots. "If you work alone," he said, "you will miss the story." His observation still holds. Lone voices drift.

The digital creator often feels they must carry everything themselves: research, production, delivery, pastoral care, and crisis management. But the solitary posture extracts a hidden cost. Without colleagues who ask difficult questions, the leader's voice begins to warp. Precision erodes, tone sharpens, and motives blur. Problems appear first at the edges: uncorrected factual slips, late-night posts made in frustration, or unacknowledged strain that spills into public replies. The algorithms do not warn you. Your audience rarely does. Only the team does. This is the trellis motif again—the frame that keeps growth upright. Without it, the vine wanders into places never intended.

Examples across disciplines illustrate the point. In 2019, the historian Jill Lepore described her editorial circle at *The New Yorker*, where each long-form essay passes through a team responsible for verifying claims line by line, questioning narrative choices, and probing whether an argument has drifted from evidence to conjecture. Lepore credits this circle with preserving not only accuracy but balance, ensuring that no single emotional impulse steers the entire piece. The visible behaviour is forensic checking: footnotes traced, emails examined, quotes confirmed. The implication is cultural rather than procedural—truth becomes a shared obligation, not the burden of an isolated writer.

A second example comes from outside publishing. In 2017, the charity Christian Aid introduced an internal peer-review panel for public statements, including those made on social media. Each draft passed before three colleagues: one to assess theological integrity, one to evaluate pastoral sensitivity, and one to consider reputational risk. Results were measurable. Within a year, the organisation reported a 40 per cent drop in posts requiring later clarification or apology (Christian Aid, 2018). The metric is crude but revealing. Accountability did not slow the team; it steadied them.

Yet accountability circles carry a limitation that demands attention. When created poorly, they devolve into echo chambers. Some groups become so socially tight or financially entangled that scrutiny weakens. Members hesitate to challenge a leader whose approval they depend on. This pattern has surfaced in several high-profile digital ministries during the past decade, where teams existed in name but not function. Ideas sailed through unchallenged, and crises unfolded in public. The reconciliation requires intentional structure: independence of members, clarity about authority, and norms that encourage candour even when uncomfortable. A trellis that bends too easily cannot hold weight.

At the heart of team accountability sits a simple behaviour: asking the questions the audience cannot. A colleague who reviews tone might say, "Why are you responding this way?" or "What unseen frustration shaped these words?" A theological reviewer might ask, "Is this interpretation faithful to the tradition you stand within?" A wellbeing observer might ask, "Why were you online at 1:47 a.m.?"

These are not abstract notions of trust or risk but concrete interventions at specific times and in visible habits. Questions become mirrors. Mirrors sharpen sight.

The work becomes more complex when addressing conflict. In 2021, the interfaith project Scriptural Reasoning UK recorded that its discussion groups remained civil not because participants were uniformly polite but because each session included a facilitator trained to interrupt spirals, summarise points of tension, and redirect energy constructively. The facilitator's presence altered behaviour: fewer interruptions, more citations of primary texts, and greater willingness to sit with disagreement. Accountability, in this sense, becomes choreographic—shaping not only what is said but how it is said. The team holds the space.

The digital creator often imagines that such structures belong only to formal institutions, yet informal circles can be equally effective. A small group that meets fortnightly for one hour can transform a leader's public posture. The visible behaviours include reading drafts aloud before posting, reviewing analytics with suspicion rather than pride, and discussing whether a recent reaction aligns with the creator's stated commitments. This is the slow work of recalibration. It looks undramatic, almost trivial. But small corrections prevent large deviations.

A mild counter-example shows the tension. Some creators, frustrated by committee slowness, abandon teams altogether and work alone "for clarity." For a season, output may indeed appear cleaner—fewer meetings, faster publication, tighter control. But in several documented cases from 2012–2020 across digital activism and online education, scholars observed a pattern: the solitary leader gradually became less accurate, less responsive to critique, and more convinced of their own indispensability. Meetings had delayed them; teams had protected them. The trellis again—visibly unnecessary until the moment the plant collapses.

Accountability also matters for wellbeing. Research by the Centre for Humane Technology (2020) found that creators who operate without relational boundaries experience significantly higher burnout rates. The variable was not workload but isolation.

Colleagues functioned as shock absorbers, absorbing emotional weight and offering perspective in moments of strain. Without them, leaders internalised every complaint and crisis. The metric was startling: creators with consistent team contact reported burnout symptoms at roughly half the rate of those working alone. The behaviour that correlated most strongly was simple—weekly check-ins of at least fifteen minutes.

A team shapes not only tone and health but motive. Oversight circles often ask the questions no algorithm will: "Why are you posting this now?" "What outcome are you hoping for?" "What fear is driving this?" These questions dismantle the illusion that public communications emerge from neutral space. Lone voices drift because no one interrogates the undercurrent. When motives are explored in safe settings, public work becomes cleaner, less defensive, and more rooted in service than in visibility. This is where accountability shades into pastoral care.

The motif that returns throughout this subchapter is the watchtower. A tower is unnecessary when the landscape is calm, but when storms arrive—or when the horizon warps—its height reveals what the ground obscures. A team functions as a watchtower for the creator: seeing wider, earlier, and more clearly. Without that elevated perspective, the leader stands exposed to gusts they cannot measure. With it, they navigate storms that would otherwise uproot them.

Accountability also dignifies failure. In 2015, the writer Ta-Nehisi Coates noted that his early drafts only became coherent because trusted readers were willing to tell him which passages were weak, which arguments sagged, and which emotions clouded clarity. Their criticism stung, yet he insisted it was the only reason the work endured. The implication is uncomfortable: if your team cannot wound your pride in private, the public will wound your credibility in full view.

But there is a final tension. Accountability demands vulnerability. Vulnerability risks exposure. Exposure requires trust. And trust, once broken, is slow to rebuild. Some creators hesitate to form teams because they fear betrayal or misinterpretation. The fear is not groundless; history offers examples where internal critique became external scandal. The reconciliation lies in structure: confidentiality agreements, shared expectations, and careful selection of colleagues who have demonstrated integrity over time. Trust is measured in years, not weeks.

This subchapter edges toward a sharper question, one that cannot be dodged: who watches your work before the world does? The feed values speed. Integrity requires inspection. Momentum rewards impulse. Wisdom requires interruption. A creator who intends to serve a community must choose which voice governs their decisions—theirs alone, or theirs in concert with others who see what they cannot. The choice is unavoidable, the cost unavoidable, and the consequences—good or ill—unmistakable.

And yet the unresolved tension remains: how many guards does a watchtower need before it becomes a fortress? How much scrutiny strengthens a voice before it stifles it? How can a leader remain accountable without becoming dependent? These are questions no team can answer for you. They must be lived, measured, and revisited as the work grows. The trellis, the tower, the team—each holds its place. The drift begins the moment the creator imagines they can walk alone.

Measuring What Matters: Define fruit beyond views

In April 2016, staff at the Corrymeela Community in Ballycastle, Northern Ireland, reviewed a year of digital and in-person reconciliation work. Their public videos had drawn impressive numbers—one clip surpassed 300,000 views within forty-eight hours—but the metric that shaped their annual report was not reach but repair. They counted thirty-three facilitated conversations between families divided by legacy violence, twelve cross-community youth retreats, and seventeen documented reconciliations where people who had avoided each other for years agreed to speak again. The report listed these numbers alongside stories of fragile, slow progress. It made no mention of the most viral clip. Corrymeela's director, Donna Hicks, put it simply: "A view is not a conversion. A click is not a commitment." Her distinction named a deeper paradox. Digital creators sit before dashboards that quantify everything except what they most hope to cultivate.

Creators feel this tension every time analytics spike. A short video or post spreads quickly, yet nothing in the chart reveals whether it sparked generosity, shifted habits, or softened hostilities. The platform offers bars, lines, and heat maps, but no measure of patience gained, resentment released, or service begun. This absence is not neutral. It shapes behaviour. The mind drifts towards whatever can be counted, and what can be counted is rarely what communities prize. If fruit is defined by visibility alone, then the unseen withers. If success lives only in exposure, then fidelity quietly erodes. The trellis motif returns: structure directs growth; measurement directs motive.

A more grounded model arises from community health work. In 2004, Partners In Health tracked not only the number of patients reached in rural Haiti but specific acts of accompaniment—visits, shared meals, hours spent walking with individuals who had no transport. These were behaviours, not abstractions; they had dates, durations, and names. The implication was decisive: impact expanded because attention expanded. When the organisation measured presence rather than publicity, staff prioritised presence. Digital creators face the same choice. What we measure becomes what we perform.

The first major claim demands a concrete example: the choice to privilege testimonies over traffic. In 2018, the Jesuit Refugee Service in Rome redesigned its public reporting. Instead of ranking posts by reach, it began collecting narrative feedback from displaced families who participated in educational programmes. Staff recorded how many individuals sought legal advice after reading a guidance thread, how many enrolled in language classes following a livestream, and how many returned to volunteer. The visible behaviour was simple: calling or meeting participants after engagements, asking direct questions, taking careful notes. Within a year, enrolment in support initiatives rose by 22 per cent (JRS Annual Review, 2019). The metric shifted; the ministry shifted with it.

A second example comes from the British activist collective Citizens UK. In London in 2020, during community listening campaigns held partly online due to pandemic restrictions, organisers tracked not retweets but relational depth. They counted one-to-one conversations, recorded who followed up with whom, and identified moments when fractured neighbourhood groups began discussing shared goals. The behaviour was observable—names, dates, places. And when the collective assessed its year, it highlighted not the reach of its digital materials but the number of new civic partnerships formed (thirty-nine across six boroughs). The implication is stark: relational metrics predict change more reliably than attention metrics.

But limitations exist. A counter-example shows the complexity. Some creators who shift entirely away from quantitative measures risk drifting into sentimentality. They trust only stories, but stories can mislead. A handful of glowing messages can mask broader confusion; a moving testimony can conceal doctrinal slippage or unacknowledged harm. Without some numerical indicators—frequency, retention, participation—leaders may mistake intensity for breadth. That error is reconcilable only by pairing qualitative and quantitative measures, allowing the two to interrogate each other. When the numbers run ahead of the stories, the creator must ask why. When the stories outshine the numbers, the creator must test whether impact is real or romanticised.

The second major claim: visible behaviours reveal "fruit" more accurately than digital noise. Fruit must be caught in the act. Hours volunteered, conflicts mediated, patterns sustained across months—these expose the health of a community. A livestream expression of gratitude means little unless it corresponds to later choices: commitments kept, habits changed. The Jewish philosopher Martin Buber emphasised the *I–Thou* encounter as the site of transformation. The modern equivalent might be a recorded behaviour: who turned up for a difficult conversation, who apologised publicly, who contributed time to a service project. These acts are measurable without being reductive. They trace character in motion.

The motif of the ledger becomes useful here. A ledger is structured, deliberate, honest. But not every ledger records what matters. Digital creators keep ledgers of engagement, but few keep ledgers of repair. Imagine a creator who notes each instance of reconciliation that emerged after a conflict—names withheld, circumstances summarised, outcomes tracked. Imagine another who records when a teaching prompted local acts of service: hours spent tutoring, meals delivered, neighbours helped. These are metrics with weight because they map consequence, not attention. They reveal the shape of change.

Yet metrics alone cannot capture interior transformation. The limitation is unavoidable. No dashboard measures whether a teaching softened arrogance or humbled a leader. No spreadsheet captures whether a creator resisted the temptation to reply sharply late at night. These matters, though unquantifiable, are not unobservable. They appear in tone over time, in the pace of replies, in the restraint of not posting. A team—discussed earlier in this chapter—can observe these patterns even when numbers cannot. The ledger motif accommodates this: some entries contain numbers; others contain notes.

Another major claim concerns the distortive effect of platform incentives. In 2022, a study by the Reuters Institute examined how religious and civic educators adjusted their content towards algorithmic favourability. The findings showed measurable shifts: shorter videos, more reactive posts, and increased emotional intensity. The visible behaviours changed first; the theology or ethical posture shifted after. The implication is unavoidable. If fruit is defined by reach, reach will eventually reshape the message. Measuring beyond views is not a moral luxury but a structural necessity to preserve integrity.

What, then, should creators track? Two forms of evidence help. First, documented testimonies gathered at intervals—quarterly or biannually—tracking not emotional reactions but decisions taken: debt repaid, grudges addressed, commitments renewed. These testimonies need not be public; often they should not be. Second, patterns of communal participation: attendance in shared practices, frequency of follow-up engagement, willingness to contribute rather than merely consume. These metrics focus on reciprocity rather than volume. They expose whether a community is forming or merely watching.

A further example returns to the trellis motif. In 2015, the Taizé Community in France introduced digital reflections that complemented their in-person gatherings. Post-implementation review did not examine video views; it counted how many participants later volunteered in local peacebuilding teams. The behaviour measured—hours of service—connected the digital reflection to grounded action. When the number rose, the community attributed growth not to messaging style but to clarity of invitation. Structure supported flourishing.

The counter-example to this approach surfaces among creators who mistake busyness for fruitfulness. They track internal labour—posts delivered, drafts written, hours streamed—rather than external consequence. The reconciliation lies in asking which behaviours correspond to health. In 2021, youth leaders in Manchester shifted from counting event attendance to counting mentoring hours. The effect was immediate: far fewer events, far deeper relationships. Fruit bloomed in the quiet, not in the crowded.

Across all these cases, the question reappears: what is the ledger for? A ledger that tracks only what can be monetised—views, clicks, conversions—eventually impoverishes the creator's vision. A ledger that tracks only what feels good results in drift. The creator must choose metrics that reveal commitments kept, relationships strengthened, and growth sustained over time. These metrics require work: calls made, surveys designed, testimonies archived, service logged. Fruit becomes tangible because someone cared enough to count.

Variation across traditions adds depth. In the Benedictine order, the rule requires monks to examine their conduct daily, naming specific acts of humility, service, or transgression. This practice is not introspective for its own sake; it grounds the community in shared memory and mutual accountability. Digital creators can adapt a similar rhythm: weekly or monthly periods of reflection on specific behaviours—how many conflicts were resolved, how many people received support, how many decisions were made slowly rather than impulsively. The quiet motif returns: the ledger reveals what the heart values.

But the unresolved tension persists. If creators measure only long-term fruit, they may neglect the small signals of encouragement that sustain them. If they measure too many subtle behaviours, they risk drowning in data. If they measure too little, they risk drifting into self-satisfaction or despair. The practical trade-off becomes sharp: which metrics shape fidelity rather than vanity? Which numbers guide, and which numbers seduce?

This leads to the concluding movement. A creator committed to meaningful work must ask a diagnostic question that no platform dashboard will pose: if all views vanished tomorrow, what evidence would remain that your work bore fruit? The answer cannot be guessed; it must be found in behaviours, recorded with care. And then, a harder question follows: which of these evidences will you choose to count, and which will you allow to remain unseen so that they retain their sacredness?

Seasons, Endings, and Legacy: Know when to pause or pass the mic

In July 2014, at the Iona Community's annual gathering on the Isle of Mull, its then-leader, John Bell, stepped back from a decade of public teaching to enter a planned sabbatical. The announcement surprised many participants; Bell's music and liturgy shaped the community's rhythm, and his absence felt inconceivable. Yet the sabbatical was not a failure of energy but an act of discipline. Two months later, during the autumn meetings in Glasgow, the community reported a rise in participation from younger members who had previously remained quiet. Bell later described the period as "a necessary winter that allowed other roots to strengthen." His phrasing captured a deeper truth: creative authority carries a season, and wise leadership ends its season before it collapses.

The digital creator faces a sharper version of that question. Platforms reward constancy—daily uploads, relentless presence, perpetual commentary. Yet the human voice cannot sustain perpetual summer. Fatigue distorts judgement; burnout corrodes tone. A creator may continue to publish long after the inner well has run dry. This mismatch becomes visible in small ways: sharper replies, hurried posts, reduced curiosity. These signs function like the first yellowing of leaves—a signal that the season is shifting whether the creator acknowledges it or not.

The motif of the season frames the first claim: endings, when chosen deliberately, protect communities. The claim must be shown, named, explained, and applied. Consider the example of Krista Tippett, who in 2021 paused her long-running *On Being* project for a structured redesign. She announced the pause with exact dates and a defined process: six months of discernment, team consultation, and public reflection. The concrete behaviour mattered—she published a timetable, held Q&A sessions, and asked listeners for feedback on future direction. When the programme returned in spring 2022, its scope had narrowed but its influence deepened. The implication is clear. A planned winter replenishes the soil.

The second example comes from the Shadhili Sufi order in Morocco. In 1985, its then-guide, Sidi Hamza al-Qadiri, instituted a practice of rotational teaching. Senior disciples took turns leading weekly gatherings while he retreated for extended periods of silence. The dates, names, and gatherings are documented in the order's records held in Madagh. The visible behaviour—scheduled withdrawal—allowed both authority and humility to coexist. Younger teachers developed their voices in his absence; the community gained depth that depended on no single figure. When measured over decades, this practice prevented the cult of personality that has fractured many spiritual groups.

But a limitation must be acknowledged. Pauses and succession can unsettle communities that feel fragile. Too abrupt a departure can create confusion or even betrayal. A counter-example comes from a widely followed online teacher in 2019 whose sudden disappearance—no explanation, no timeline—left followers anxious and speculating. Some assumed crisis; others assumed scandal. The silence damaged trust, not because of the break itself, but because the break lacked form. This does not invalidate the principle of seasons; it clarifies it. Rest must be named, timed, and contextualised.

The next claim concerns legacy and the visible decisions that shape it. Legacy sounds grand, but in practice it is measurable: who continues the work, how well they do it, and whether the community retains coherence when the founder steps back. The behaviour that signals healthy legacy-building is the deliberate passing of specific responsibilities—moderation, teaching, coordination—to others long before crisis demands it. The motif of the season returns here: spring is preparation, summer is flourishing, autumn is handover, winter is rest.

One named example is the succession model of the Taizé Community. When Brother Roger founded the community in 1940, he wrote into its early documents that leadership would eventually transition to Brother Alois. The plan became public when Alois assumed leadership in August 2005. Because the decision had been prepared years earlier, the transition occurred without rupture. The visible behaviours—shared leadership in worship, joint appearances, collective decision-making—had already normalised the change. The implication for digital creators is straightforward. If a community depends entirely on one voice, its season will be short.

Another example appears in the work of activist Grace Lee Boggs in Detroit. By the 1990s, she intentionally stepped back from leading demonstrations and instead invested her time mentoring younger organisers. Her recorded interviews from 2012–14 show a consistent phrase: "The next revolution requires new hands." She hosted small study groups, co-wrote teaching materials, and insisted that younger leaders take the microphone at public events. These behaviours preserved continuity while encouraging mutation—a necessary combination if a movement is to outlive its founders.

But legacy also carries risk. The counter-example arises when leaders cling too tightly, mistaking longevity for faithfulness. Some creators maintain control over tone, content, and direction long after their judgement has narrowed. They may fear dilution or misinterpretation, yet the refusal to share authority yields a predictable pattern: stagnation followed by fragmentation.

Reconciling this limitation requires a difficult virtue—trust. Trust expressed not in vague sentiment but in concrete actions: giving others editing rights, sharing passwords transparently within an oversight circle, allowing someone else to lead major conversations.

A third claim concerns endings as acts of care. The behaviour that exhibits this truth is intentional closure. Whether it is a sabbatical, a temporary freeze, or a final handover, healthy endings require clarity. A creator must state the reason, the duration, and the expectations. When the Church of England's media team paused its *Faith Online* series in June 2020, it published a short notice outlining three steps: an audit of digital tone, a consultation with parish leaders, and a scheduled return in September. The precision protected trust. Viewers understood what was happening and why. Suspicion had no space to germinate.

Endings without clarity breed suspicion; clarity without compassion breeds coldness. The balance is found in pace. Communities can absorb change if given time to adjust. They struggle when change arrives overnight. Thus the recurrent motif—the season—guides behaviour. Seasons do not shift in an instant; they turn slowly, with signs. A creator who recognises these signs—faltering attention, rising irritation, shrinking imagination—must treat them not as failures but as forecasts. They signal the approach of winter, not its arrival. Winter invites rest, learning, repair.

The next claim: passing the mic is not abdication but multiplication. The behaviour that illustrates this is co-leadership. Sharing streams, co-teaching, hosting dialogues—these visibly transfer authority. In 2022, a popular educator in Nairobi, Pastor Janet Mbugua, restructured her digital ministry by inviting three younger women to co-host weekly reflections. Each host took responsibility for a distinct theme: justice, family life, and spiritual practice. Metrics from her public channel showed a slight decline in initial views but a steady rise in sustained engagement across six months. More importantly, stories emerged of local study groups led by those younger women. Influence became distributed. The implication is unmistakable. Passing the mic multiplies the work.

Yet a limitation appears when leaders attempt to pass the mic but fail to prepare successors. Without preparation, new voices feel exposed and unsupported. Succession demands mentoring—scheduled meetings, shared decision logs, joint moderation sessions. These visible acts demonstrate commitment. Without them, passing the mic becomes abandonment. Reconciliation occurs when creators recognise that preparation takes longer than relinquishment. A slow, steady transfer of responsibility allows trust to develop.

Another dimension concerns the creator's inner life. The season motif applies here as well. No one can remain perpetually outward-facing. The Jewish practice of *shmita*—a sabbatical year every seven years—exemplifies a rhythm of pausing production to restore land and community. Its behaviour is explicit: fields rest, debts pause, relationships reset. Digital creators might adopt an analogue: a scheduled year or quarter when output slows, reflection deepens, and internal recalibration occurs. The implication is restorative. Without these rhythms, the soil erodes.

A further claim: endings reveal character. How a creator steps back—graciously, transparently, or defensively—shapes the community's memory far more than any single piece of content. The behaviour that demonstrates this truth is gratitude. Publicly acknowledging collaborators, naming mistakes, and honouring those who supported the work gives the community permission to remember the creator with warmth rather than anxiety. Legacy is measured not by the number of followers retained but by the quality of relationships sustained.

Yet the unresolved tension remains. If a creator steps back too early, vital work may stall. If they step back too late, they may damage what they built. If they pass the mic carelessly, they may endanger the community's cohesion. If they hold it too tightly, they may suffocate growth. There is no formula, only discernment. And discernment requires both solitude and counsel—quiet reflection and honest feedback.

This subchapter ends, deliberately, with a question rather than an answer. When the season turns—and it always turns—what gesture will ensure that your community not only survives your pause but flourishes because of it?

About the Author

Liora Ben-Sorrel writes at the meeting point of tradition and technology, exploring how sacred practices adapt to networked life. Her work focuses on attention, integrity, and community in digital spaces, drawing on long-form conversations with leaders, educators, and creators across diverse faith settings. She is interested in how design choices shape belief and behaviour, and how small, consistent habits outlast noise. A subtle thread runs through her thinking: the continuity between wandering teachers, printing press preachers, radio chaplains, and today's livestream mentors. She brings a steady, practical voice to a noisy field, translating ancient wisdom into workable patterns for modern platforms.

www.ingramcontent.com/pod-product-compliance
Lightning Source LLC
Chambersburg PA
CBHW031344230926
51848CB00002B/376